T0072168

EDIBLE

EDIBLE

An Adventure into the World
of Eating Insects
and the Last Great Hope
to Save the Planet

Daniella Martin

amazonpublishing

Published by Amazon Publishing, Seattle

www.apub.com

Amazon and the Amazon logo are trademarks of Amazon.com, Inc. or its affiliates.

ISBN: 9781477822524

Jacket designed by Rodrigo Corral Design
Author photograph by James Rollyson

Printed in the United States of America

For Brian, my smizmar

Contents

EDIBLE

Introduction

THIS BOOK IS about eating bugs. For real. And if you make it all the way through the book, you're going to want to taste the revolution for yourself.

Why? Eating bugs* makes sense — ecological, nutritional, economic, global, and culinary sense. Yes, they even taste good. Many people disdainfully say they "don't like bugs," are afraid of them, or are repelled by them on some deep, subconscious, yet stridently self-righteous level. But like them or not, insects are the largest terrestrial biomass on Earth. That means of all the animals that live on dry land, insects are most of them. If someone were to determine, by the numbers, what Earth was about, they would conclude: insects. Beetles, mostly.

Consider the fact that the planet you live on has more bugs on it than any other animal (I know, it's making your

---

* The terms "bug" and "insect" will be used interchangeably throughout this book to mean "terrestrial invertebrate." This can include arthropods, annelids, and gastropods — essentially any terrestrial invertebrate not generally considered edible by Westerners.

skin crawl just thinking about it). Insects were here before us, and they'll help us decompose after we die. People say money makes the world go round, which may be true within human society, but in nature, it's bugs. Bugs do the majority of the pollinating and decomposing, the real circle of life. And that's not to mention how important pollination is for the food we grow and eat. The bugs we love to hate—like bees, wasps, and even mosquitoes—all contribute to pollination, which helps begin life. Decomposition, largely performed by insects, dismantles it, making room for more life to flourish. And yet we tend to treat them as a whole as if they are worse than the garbage certain species help decompose.

This is a large part of the reason I am so inspired by insects, why I've spent nearly a decade thinking about them and studying them, and why I wrote this book. I truly believe we should all be eating bugs—as our ancestors did, as our global neighbors do, as our primate cousins do, and as we ourselves do constantly, by accident, without realizing it.

I'm not asking anyone to drastically change their diet, to give up foods they love, or to subscribe to some new overarching system. I'm not even going to suggest substituting insects in place of other foods, per se. I'm simply asking you to open your mind—just a little—to give bugs a chance and a place on your palate.

Whenever anyone finds out for the first time just what it is I do, the first thing they want to know is "How did you get into *that?*"

The first time I ever ate a bug, on purpose, was in Oaxaca, Mexico. I was traveling on a student visa, studying pre-Columbian food and medicine for my BA in cultural anthropology. Mainly, I wanted to see what vestiges of early Mexican life had survived the Spanish conquistadors, and their systematic squelching of native practices, into modern-day life. I'd read about entomophagy—insect eating—in college, how the ancient Aztecs and Maya ate everything that was available to them, including insects, rodents, and reptiles. If it moved, they ate it. And often to great success—there were stories about how, during the right season, a person could wade into Lake Tenochtitlan, the center of the Aztec world, with a couple of agave-fiber nets and come back with twenty to thirty pounds of larvae and other aquatic insects within a few hours. That might not sound so great to us, but when compared with the difficulties, dangers, and unreliability of hunting, it's a pretty darn awesome return on investment. That's a big load of high-quality protein, fats, minerals, and vitamins for remarkably little effort, energy, and risk.

I knew when I went to Mexico that I was definitely going to have to try edible insects for myself. It was also one of the few easily observable practices that was a clear holdover from earlier times. Certainly, there are many foods that remain as popular today in Mexico as they were when they were first cultivated and developed by the Aztecs: corn tortillas, tamales, beans, chiles. But the historic purity of many of these foods is somewhat diluted with modern ingredients, such as lard, and modern processing machines. Insects, however, are often eaten just as they were thousands of years ago: dried in the sun, toasted on a comal (a flat, earthenware cooking surface), or ground up in a *molcajete*, a mortar and pestle carved from volcanic rock, one of the world's oldest kitchen tools. In the cities, insects are generally deemed a delicacy (and their price reflects this), but in the countryside, where the majority of native people live, they are more a way of life. For me, this lent them a certain wholeness as an unbroken tie to the past—

and thus anthropologically interesting in terms of my goal of recording the modern life of ancient traditions.

When I saw a middle-aged woman, dressed in a brightly colored Mayan wrap, selling toasted grasshoppers in the Oaxaca city square, it was a no-brainer. I paid my 20 pesos and received a little paper bag of the brick-red bugs. I took my roasted grasshoppers, called *chapulines*, and sat down at a table in an outdoor café. I was definitely going to need something to wash this down with. I ordered a Coke and poured the *chapulines* out onto the white tablecloth, intending to take a cool photograph before sampling them. Just as I was getting ready to brave my first bite of bug, the strangest thing happened: Kids from the street, likely of Trique indigenous descent, made a beeline for me and began eating the *chapulines* right off my table—without even asking! I hardly had time to grab a few for myself, as they gobbled them right up.

Now, I've thought about this in the years since it happened: Yes, the kids were likely hungry—more than 70 percent of Oaxacans live in extreme poverty. These children spend their days begging tourists on the streets of the city while their parents sell various things in the market: *elotes*, a chili-spiced corn on the cob; indigenous crafts and trinkets; and, of course, toasted insects. The kids had probably seen lots of tourists buy a bag of *chapulines* "for the experience," eat one or two, squinch up their faces, take a few photos, and throw the rest away. The kids must have supposed, "Eh, she won't care, she's a tourist. Let's get 'em while the getting's good, while they're still crispy and we don't have to fish them out of the trash." On the one hand, it could be interpreted as a bit Dickensian; on the other, Cheetos are technically made of yuckier stuff than this.

I managed to taste a few *chapulines*, and I probably would

have thrown the rest away. They tasted unfamiliar, sort of like a shriveled, spicy, slightly burned potato chip, but mostly, the mind gets in the way, telling you it won't be safe or good to eat too many. Heck, you might turn into a bug yourself (Dickens meets Kafka?). But there are lots of foods I love that others are slightly grossed out by: beef tongue, smelly fermented soybeans, tinned sardines and oysters, oily raw mackerel, and all manner of fish eggs. So why not bugs?

What struck me was that it seemed like the kids were eating them because they liked them. They genuinely wanted to eat them, just like American kids want to eat Cheetos.

Over the years, I have seen plenty of well-fed kids happily eat handfuls of bugs, usually when their parents aren't looking. One four-year-old boy ate more than two dozen of my sautéed larvae at a demonstration in Georgia, until his mother physically dragged him away, still chewing. He had been literally (and hilariously) shoving other kids out of the way to get his hands on the mothling morsels. A six-year-old in Niagara Falls, Canada, ate six big fried crickets to the shock and awe of the audience and her conservative Indian family. I've had kids sneak back for seconds, thirds, fourths, and beyond, happily crunching away behind their parents' backs. While prepping for a television shoot in San Francisco for KQED, the Bay Area's PBS member station, one crew member's six-year-old daughter ate half a dozen toasted mealworms and crickets before the cameras were even turned on.

These kids aren't eating bugs for the shock effect. They're not doing it for photos they can post on their Facebook pages. They're doing it because the bugs taste good and because the idea that bugs are bad hasn't yet solidified in their as yet unsocialized, unossified minds. I think there might be a delicious, subversive thrill in it for them as well. Here they are taking something their parents tell them is gross, dirty, and dangerous—and eating it! Children are still wild inside. They still have one foot in the mud, in the savanna, in the jungle. We civilize, socialize, and organize them, just as we have other wild, bug-loving cultures, and by the time most of them are adults, that open curiosity and trust of nature has been largely Purelled out of them.

Children are usually delighted when I tell them they can eat bugs. They are so naturally curious and open and unafraid that the idea of eating a bug seems like a great new experience they can't wait to have. When they find out the bugs actually taste good, it's like icing on the cake. They feel, I think, the way I felt when I found out bugs could be edible: as if someone had opened a whole new door of possibility to me. You know those little things that are everywhere, abundant, tiny, and colorful? Not only are they cool to look at, but you can *eat* 'em, too.

I didn't get into studying entomophagy right away after that first experience in Mexico. It remained just one part of my thesis, but it was the part that fascinated me most. I had no idea until several years later that there was actually a movement in the world, a small group of passionate individuals, working to bring this ancient idea into modern Western culture.

In 2008, I happened to read an article in *Time* magazine* chronicling an edible insect cookoff in Richmond, Virginia, between bug chefs David George Gordon and David Gracer. It also mentioned a Food and Agriculture Organization–sponsored edible insect conference that had taken place recently in Thailand. The article discussed new research on

---

* Brian Walsh, "Eating Bugs," *Time*, May 29, 2008.

insects as a possible global food source, a potential solution to world hunger, and an eco-friendly alternative to beef and other livestock. I was stunned, thrilled. Here I was, privately fascinated by this little-known practice, and it was being taken seriously by international organizations. There were people quoted in this article who lived in America, who actually took this stuff seriously. And not only that, but people elsewhere in the world, in powerful positions at the Food and Agriculture Organization (FAO) of the United Nations, who saw the potential in edible insects. This could be a real thing.

At that moment, I realized the first thing I had to do, obviously, was to start cooking bugs for myself.

As you can imagine, it was an intimidating process. Despite my love of intensely flavored foods, I am a cautious person, a bit of a hypochondriac, and gastrointestinally sensitive. I'm allergic to alcohol and lactose intolerant, and breakfast cereal has been known to give me a stomachache. So where does one begin if one wants to eat something as unusual and traditionally reviled as bugs?

I ordered *The Eat-a-Bug Cookbook: 33 Ways to Cook Grasshoppers, Ants, Water Bugs, Spiders, Centipedes, and Their Kin* by David George Gordon. Although it's written in a lighthearted style, it was clear the man had done his research on the subject, in addition to writing several other books on biological topics. Next I ordered *Creepy Crawly Cuisine: The Gourmet Guide to Edible Insects* by Julieta Ramos-Elorduy, a Mexican biologist who focuses on native entomophagy. The traditional Mexican recipes complemented the American *Eat-a-Bug Cookbook*, and armed with both, I set about my goal. Since I'd already tried prepared insects, I wanted to experiment with fresh ones. The only way to really do this, I soon learned, was to order them live.

Where could a person order live, edible insects? Which kinds were available that I'd actually want to eat? It turns out that the best sources for live insects are bug farms, which raise their stock primarily to sell to pet owners, particularly those who own reptiles. Put simply, I was going to be eating lizard food.

The backgrounds of these bugs plagued me. For a woman who adores taco trucks and will happily eat a hot dog of suspicious origins from a street vendor (yes, I'm a bit contradictory. I'm careful yet intrepid. Isn't that what you want in a bug-eater?), I was uncharacteristically concerned with how these bugs had been raised. So I started making phone calls. I came right out with it, asking if various insect stock was safe for human consumption. What did they eat?

I received a variety of not-exactly-comforting answers— "They eat cricket feed," "We use mainly dog food," or, sometimes, "You want to do *what* with them?"—until I called San Diego Wax Worms. "Oh yes," said the woman on the phone. "My husband occasionally eats them raw right out of the bins." Bingo. It wasn't an answer I could take to the bank, but it seemed like a start. After all, I intended to cook the little buggers.

I ordered 250 live wax worms and waited in nervous anticipation. Wax worms are the larvae, or caterpillars, of the wax moth. In the wild, they live in beehives, eating bee leftovers and pollen and tunneling through the wax, which is how they get their name (imagine Pac-Man in a honeycomb). Naturally, they are a bane to beekeepers but a boon to the beekeepers' chickens, if they have any. In captivity, they are raised on a diet of bran and honey. Wax worms sounded like a pretty good bet to me.

They arrived in a box covered in LIVE ANIMAL alerts—I hoped my landlord hadn't been too suspicious. Inside there was a small blue plastic container with tiny airholes punched in the top. I opened it up to find a pile of wood shavings (included to pad the hard, exoskeleton-less bodies) and tiny, wriggling, cream-colored larvae. Kind of like a maggot, but more beige and bigger. I picked one up. It was squishy. It had a tiny black head and six little feet like the nipples on a dog. It squirmed out of my tentative grasp and burrowed back down into the safety of the shavings.

I had read that the best way to prepare insects for cooking was to freeze them first. It was strangely disheartening to put these defenseless, if wriggling, babies into the freezer to their deaths, but I braced myself, said a little prayer, shoved them in and shut the door.

Several hours later, I returned, ready to roll. Fresh out of the freezer, the wax worms were like hard little pellets, reminiscent of big seeds. You have to separate them from their substrate, the wood shavings, which I did by spreading the whole mess out on a stretch of wax paper. I had to work quickly, because as they thawed, their soft bodies became more difficult to pick out.

I soon had a pile of little beige caterpillars, which I tossed in a colander to rinse off any remaining sawdust. Now it was time to get cooking. I sautéed some chopped onions until they were golden and, dubiously, dumped in the pile of wax worms.

They began to sizzle and react as they hit the pan. I kept them moving, fascinated by how their little bodies stretched out and straightened in the heat. And they smelled, for all the world, just like mushrooms.

My boyfriend at the time didn't agree. "It smells weird, like, earthy or something," Nick said, crinkling up his nose and backing out of the kitchen. This from a man who had a degree in Chinese medicine and had lived in China, who routinely ordered the more obscure organ meats at ethnic restaurants.

"Well, mushrooms are earthy," I said.

"It still smells weird," he said, though to this day I believe that was his mental bias talking. I really couldn't detect a difference, and I have a sensitive schnoz.

The wax worms were now beginning to turn golden and translucent around the edges, just like onions do when they're done. I picked one up out of the pan with a pair of chopsticks, blew on it, gingerly squeezed it between two fingers, and put it in my mouth.

Hmm. It was chewy, like a warm, savory raisin. Also buttery and nutty, with a hint of the mushroom I'd been smelling—like long, slender Japanese enoki mushrooms, to be exact. I added a bit of salt to the sauté and tried another worm. These bugs were pretty darn tasty.

"Wow," I said. "Honey, these are *good!*"

"That's nice," came the uncomfortable response from the next room.

I scooped up a bunch of the golden larvae with a spatula and put them into a corn tortilla. This was as close to native Mexican cuisine as I could conveniently come. I added some salsa, avocado slices, and a bit of cilantro. I took a big bite. Delicious! Nutty, savory, earthy, nourishing. Nothing not to like.

"These really are good, no kidding," I said to Nick. "Are you sure you don't want to taste them? One tiny bite?"

"I really don't want to," he said firmly. "I'm happy to support your doing it, but I just don't want to."

Nick was supportive; for my birthday that year, he bought me my first expensive tome on entomophagy, something many experts today don't even own, and which helped me become an expert in the field. He just didn't want to participate in the actual eating.

In the *Time* magazine article I'd read, Dave Gracer had won the bug-cooking contest with his Ant Queen, Stinkbug, and Waxworm Salad. I looked up his company, SmallStock Foods, which supplies hard-to-find edible arthropods from all over the world to people like Andrew Zimmern, host of Bizarre Foods. I gave him a ring. He was very friendly and told me to drop by the next time I was in his home state of Rhode Island, which happened to be soon.

The first time I met Dave, he generously invited me over to his house for my first bug feast. I arrived in time for dinner, and he promptly took me down to his basement, where he had an entire freezer dedicated to bugs. For the squeamish, it was like a Little Freezer of Horrors, but for me, it was as if he had opened the doors to heaven and the sound of angels singing. He had insects from all over the world, things I'd only read about in books: locusts, katydids, cockroaches, water bugs, giant ants, tiny bullet-like fly pupae, little green stinkbugs, bamboo worms, giant walking sticks, and other things in plastic bags and Tupperware containers that I couldn't identify.

For dinner that night, Dave brought out what I now realize was only a fraction of his holdings and prepared a plate for me. As a burgeoning entomophagist, this was like being a car lover and having someone hand you the keys to a garage full of Lamborghinis and Maseratis and letting you take a spin. You just can't get the kind of stuff he had in his freezeum.

I remember liking the cockroaches (he had these little ones from Colombia that he toasted up for me), and now I can tell whenever I go into a building with a roach infestation. Call it my roachy-sense. The water bug was intense. The *hormigas culonas,* "big-butt" queen ants from his supplier in Texas, were toasty and crunchy, like hollow popcorn kernels laced with beef jerky. The walking stick was awful, tasting just like leaves, which I suppose makes sense since that's what it eats. The katydids and bamboo worms were terrific, light and crispy like tiny French fries, only full of protein instead of starch. The tiny green stinkbugs were surprisingly tasty, too, with a slightly bitter, spicy vegetal bite to them, like a kale leaf.

After all those bugs, some of which had been imported from overseas, I was on high alert for digestive disturbances. My food allergies don't stop me from being adventurous, but sometimes I pay for it. I was certain that after an entire meal of exotic insects, including at least six different species, many of which were eaten whole, I'd be paying big-time. But I got off scot-free, as I have every time I've ingested the class Insecta.

By the end of that meal I had tasted more bug varieties than most people do in a lifetime—I was officially initiated into the world of entomophagy.

Since that first meeting, Dave and I have done some crazy things together: traveled to a Christian mission deep in Alabama for an international entomophagy conference, where we got to cook with the inimitable Julieta Ramos-Elorduy; eaten, among other things, dung beetles, wasps, giant cockroaches, and live termites; fried up a cave spider for a *New Yorker* reporter; competed against each other in a bug cook-off (I won that time, with my fried tarantula spider roll); wandered the private corridors of museums; presented bug dishes in Washington, DC; experimented with stinkbug cuisine in a stranger's kitchen; gone scorpion hunting with black lights at night; fed people bug snacks at the Atlanta airport.

Eating bugs makes sense, ecologically and economically. They also happen to taste really good. The more I eat insects, the more I respect them. Taking them from field or farm to plate has taught me, a recalcitrant urban-dweller, firsthand about the value of meat, and that it should never be wasted because it came from a living, breathing being not so different from us when you get right down to it. I don't believe we should clear all animal protein from our diets—partly because I've tried and it makes me feel exhausted, both mentally and physically (did you know that "brain fog" is a commonly reported symptom among vegans?)—but mostly because that's not how our ancestors or closest primate relatives approached food. They tended to eat meat when they could. Not a lot of it, and certainly not as much of it as we do, but they did eat some. We aren't ungulates, deftly digesting the cellulose in vegetable matter with giant internal fermenting tanks. We aren't carnivores, subsisting mainly off the flesh of other animals and not much else. We're omnivores by design. We eat everything—and part of that "omni" includes some animals. Why not let it be insects, whose life cycles are generally much shorter, whose resource needs are fewer, who are the most plentiful creatures on Earth, and who are already being exterminated by the millions just because we find them annoying?

Why not make the best of what we have the most of?

1

||||||||||||||||

The Problem

IMAGINE THE FAST-FOOD restaurant of the future. With environmental pressures mounting, a growing population to feed, and China calling in its mountain of American debt, farm subsidies have dwindled. Restaurants of the future have to find ways to offset the rising cost of food. Today, you've wandered into a joint with a unique approach to this problem. It's called McImpacts. Its prices are still rock bottom, but there's a catch—you have to cart off all the by-products of the meal you consume. Let's give it a whirl, shall we?

You stride up to the futuristic counter of this ultratransparent restaurant and order a burger called Trucker's Delight for reasons that aren't quite clear.

"Coming right up," says the cashier, manipulating a floating, translucent touchscreen. In less than a minute, your burger is on the counter—but behind it, the servers are unpacking the *rest* of your order: four heaping pounds of steaming cow manure, one thousand sloshing gallons of contaminated water, and a disgusting black sludge that you recognize as the carbon released by a gallon of gasoline. You hear the beeping of a heavy-duty vehicle backing up and look out the window as a huge Mack Truck pulls into view.

"What's that for?" you ask.

"That's the two hundred cubic feet of the CAFO [concentrated animal feeding operation] lot used to make your burger. It won't be good for anything else for at least a few years," says the employee. "Would you like it to go?"

You shake your head in disbelief, suddenly grasping the burger's weird name. "Is that everything?" you ask.

The employees look at one another, sigh, and put on their gas masks. The cashier pushes a button. There is an earth-shaking burp, and the air is so saturated with the smell of rotten eggs that you gag.

"That's your methane," says the cashier, her voice muffled by the gas mask. "Twenty times more potent than carbon dioxide."

You double over and retch, croaking that you'd like to change your order.

"Certainly," says the cashier cheerfully, taking off her mask. "What would you like?"

You order the McRib. Anything has to be better than this.

Out comes your sandwich, along with six hundred gallons of contaminated water. This time, there's just two and a half pounds of pig shit and a marginally smaller cloud of methane. Still gagging, you switch to the McNuggets. These turn out to be not as bad—with a ten-piece box, you get a pound of chicken feces, 150 gallons of the foulest water you've ever seen, and just a little less methane. But it's a lot to carry. Curious, you move away from terrestrial beings altogether and try the Filet-O-Fish. You begin to feel hopeful, seeing the pound of fish poop, the handful of parasites, and just ten gallons of dirty water. You could almost feel okay about ordering this—plus, you're getting hungry. As you reach for your meal, the cashier whips out a cleaver and chops the sandwich practically in half, throwing the smaller portion into the trash can.

"Forty-four percent of fish is thrown away by retailers and consumers," she says, and shrugs. Your shoulders slump; you give up. You order some fries and shuffle away.

If we were faced with the immediate consequences of our eating decisions on a daily basis, we'd quickly start asking whether they were worth it. Is eating a burger worth all this carbon, all this fouled water, all this . . . well, all this cow shit? As the human population grows, we will be directly faced with more and more of these consequences—we may never have to cart our food's by-products home from the store with us, but it can't be too much longer before we see it pile up in our backyards. When that happens, people are sure to start looking for a better option.

If farm animals are such resource hogs, why can't we all just become vegetarians? Certainly we can stand to cut out the middleman—the animals that concentrate the nutrients of plant matter in their tissues. However, many researchers suggest that concentrated animal protein is key to humans functioning at their highest level and getting the most out of life. Evolutionary biology has shown that huge jumps in human brain size coincided with increased animal protein in the diet of our evolutionary forbears. By concentrating huge amounts of energy into a tiny package, animal protein provides fuel for surprisingly calorie-intensive activities like language, critical thinking, and a rich emotional life. Furthermore, only animal protein provides the whole spectrum of amino acids essential to human biology.

Despite the vegetarian fantasy of humans subsisting solely

on plant matter, not every place in the world is conducive to growing crops. Many of the places facing the worst hunger simply do not have the right kind of land or weather, or enough water for agriculture. What are they supposed to do, wait for us to ship them our excess food? This "solution" is fraught with problems.

In fact, there is a better option—a *much* better option. If our fast-food restaurant of the future offered a McMealburger or maybe Cricket McNuggets, your side order would be a lot more palatable: about a half pound of castings nearly indistinguishable from fresh soil,* ten gallons of slightly cloudy water, no methane. A tiny smear of carbon—the energy that kept the cold-blooded insects warm.

Since most bugs don't require deboning, there are also big savings in energy and water on the processing end, and because they require far less space to raise and can thus be farmed in an urban area, the fossil fuel required to transport them is minimal. The entire impact of this meal would arrive in a tidy, reasonably sized box. In other words, if you had to personally deal with the impact, this would be the meal you would really want to eat.

As David Gracer says of the animal protein industry, "Cows and pigs are the SUVs; insects are the bicycles." Here's what the numbers look like:

> 1 pound of beef = 10 pounds of feed,[†] 1,000 gallons of
>   water, 200 square feet of pasture (2 acres per cow)
> 1 pound of pork = 5 pounds of feed, 600 gallons of water,
>   175 square feet of pasture (2/3 acre per pig)

---

* Cricket and mealworm manure is sold at a premium as plant fertilizer.
† Yes, I agree—we shouldn't be feeding cows grain, since they evolved to eat grass.

1 pound of chicken = 2.5 pounds of feed, 150 gallons of
   water, 75 square feet of pasture (100 square feet per
   chicken)
1 pound of fish = 1.5 pounds of fish meal, variable
   amounts of water, considering spawning
1 pound of insects = 2 pounds of feed, 1 gallon of water,
   2 *cubic feet* of land space

It may seem inhumane to think of animals as meat machines, but that's how we're already using them, so we might
as well be honest about it. Each of these meat machines is different. Just as a steam engine is not a combustion engine is
not a wind turbine, a cow is not a pig is not a fish. And as you
might have noticed, we don't use a whole lot of steam engines
these days.

An animal's efficiency at turning food, like grass or grain
or fish meal, into the meat that we buy is called its food
conversion ratio (FCR). If it takes two pounds of food to
make one pound of meat, the FCR is 2:1. For a steer, the ratio is approximately 10:1; for chickens, it's around 2:1. The
wide gulf in FCRs occurs because each of these animals is
working with a different physical apparatus as well as fuel
sources. Cattle take in mainly grass (or grain, in a feedlot
environment); pigs and chickens are omnivorous like we
are, eating a diet of corn, other grains, and processed animal
protein; fish are generally obligate carnivores, eating mainly
other fish.

Why does it take so much plant material to make so little beef? What makes filet mignon the blood diamond of the
livestock industry? There are a variety of factors, and it's not
as simple as cows requiring more input and releasing more ex-
haust. More important, it has to do with their basic biology,

which is vastly different from that of pigs, chickens, fish, or insects.

One thing cows can do that none of the other main live-stock breeds can do is turn otherwise inedible grass into meat. Cows can do this because they are ruminants: Their digestive systems are designed to break down plant cellulose, ideally that from grass, and turn it into protein. Humans, pigs, chickens, and fish do not have this ability at the level that cows do.

For instance, a cow's tongue—that big muscle as thick as your forearm that you might see at a butcher shop—was designed to act like a little arm, wrapping around a hunk of grass, pulling it in line with the cow's big front incisors, and then moving it to the back of the cow's mouth, so its wide molars can wrench it from side to side before sending it to the first chamber of the animal's four stomachs.

When told a cow has four stomachs, you might imagine a row of human-sized stomachs. A cow's stomach is more like one big bag, about the volume of a fifty-gallon trash can. By comparison, a human stomach holds around a half gallon. In a cow, this large stomach cavity is divided into four compartments. The main and largest compartment is the rumen, one of the most microbially dense habitats in the world. Each gram of rumen fluid contains 10–50 *billion* bacteria.

Within this huge chamber, one of the biggest parts of the animal, trillions of bacteria ferment the plants' cellulose or fiber—the part of plants that humans can't digest. In a human, this fiber serves as "roughage," which then gets excreted and helps push other material out in the process.* In a cow, the bacteria in the rumen use an enzyme called cellulase to break

---

* A.k.a. Metamucil.

the cellulose down, eat it, and in turn excrete protein from it, which the cow then absorbs and turns into hamburger. Yes, you read that right: A cow's body ultimately makes meat out of bacteria poop. I'm not trying to turn you off meat, but when it comes to judging which kinds of meat are good and which are gross, it's pretty much all equally gross.

This bacterial maneuver is a pretty impressive biological process considering the fact that outside of cows and sheep, no other livestock animal can turn grass, which humans can't eat, into meat, which we can. But turning grass into meat is also resource-intensive, and expends a lot of by-product in the form of manure and gas. The reason cows produce so much gas is precisely because of their ability to process inedible cellulose. Even cows can't directly "eat" the cellulose in grass— they require the bacteria in their rumen to do this for them. As the bacteria break down the plant fiber, methane is produced as a by-product, and the cows burp it out.* A cow burps up to 240 pounds of methane per year; as a group, cattle burp up close to 80 million metric tons of methane annually. Since methane is twenty times more potent at trapping radiation than CO_2, this amounts to 1.6 billion tons of CO_2 a year, or 30 percent more than cars produce. In terms of greenhouse gases (GHGs) that contribute to global warming, this is clearly a significant source.

In order to survive on "cheap" fuel like grass and leaves, an animal makes an evolutionary trade-off, generally one of size and metabolism. You know how a Prius doesn't go as fast as a Porsche, yet is a far more efficient vehicle? It's kind of

---

* Termites also break down cellulose when they eat wood and are, in fact, the source of 11 percent of natural (as in, not man-made) methane production worldwide. However, the important ecological role they play by breaking down rotting wood is their so-called carbon offset.

like that. On the nutrient spectrum, grass and other plants are cheap, but you have to eat more of them *and* cart around the right processing equipment to utilize them. Meat, even that from insects, is more expensive, given that it took an initial investment of something cheap like grass to make it. But a digestive system, assuming it's the right kind, can also get more mileage out of more "expensive" food.

Now, cows were designed to graze pasture, and in the right balance, they are great at this. Their particular way of eating grass, by shearing it off above the roots, actually encourages new growth. Their manure, in turn, fertilizes the soil. Done right, and in balance, pasturing cows can support and benefit a grassland ecosystem. However, when their numbers are too large, they not only overgraze the land so that it can't bounce back, but their hooves tramp down the soil, impacting it to such a degree that nothing can grow. This leads to desertification, an infertile wasteland that in many cases cannot be saved—a dire example of what our future can and will be if we don't change something, and soon.

Pigs make meat in a way very similar to humans, with digestive systems that are so much like ours that they are frequently dissected in biology classes. Pigs are monogastric, meaning they have one stomach, and omnivorous like humans, which is why they've traditionally been fed "slop"—leftovers and waste from human meals (e.g., plate scrapings and potato peelings). On modern farms, they are fed a range of carefully combined foods including corn, oats, and soy; fish, bone, and meat meal; and milk by-products (sounds good, huh?). Pigs' FCR is about 4:1; but then again, their food is of a closer quality to that of humans. Pigs, not being ruminants, aren't a direct significant source of methane like cows are, but their manure certainly is.

Chickens, also monogastric, have even simpler digestive systems. They, too, are omnivores, eating everything from grains and grasses to insects and even small rodents, and have an FCR of 2:1. For animals that lack teeth, they have a remarkably efficient digestive system. Their gizzards do all the "chewing," grinding food particles with bits of sand and gravel. Fibrous bits are sent to ferment in the cecum, which is kind of like a mini-rumen. Because they don't have the big fermenting chamber of a ruminant, chickens don't break down cellulose nearly as effectively as cows do. Chickens, like pigs, also are not big producers of methane, and, like pigs, their manure is.

That FCR of 2:1 sounds great, right? It is great; chickens are great. But what you need to factor into this number—and here's where it gets a bit complicated—is what the chicken is eating in order to get that low FCR.

Chickens, despite popular pastoral imagery, do not live on sprinkled handfuls of corn alone. They are usually fed some form of by-product mash that is generally made up of corn; ground soybean hulls from plant processing; various waste from vegetable oil production; and bits of slaughtered animals for protein and minerals, like fish meal, meat meal, bone meal, blood meal, feather meal, and "poultry by-product meal," which is ground-up chicken carcass, essentially. This latter bit is not necessarily as inhumane as it seems, since hungry chickens have been known to eat each other. In fact, chicken cannibalism may be responsible for the origin of the term "rose-colored glasses." Farmed chickens, aroused by the sight of blood on one of their coop-mates, have been known to peck that chicken to death; the losses were significant enough that tiny, red-lensed chicken glasses were sold to farmers in the early twentieth century. The glasses, attached to the beak via a bar through the nostrils, made it so the chickens couldn't see blood but could still see grain. They have since been banned on animal cruelty grounds; meanwhile, beak trimming via a heated blade remains today's answer to the problem.

The animal protein in chicken mash substitutes for the myriad insects the chickens would naturally be pecking from their environment if they were strutting around a sunny field as chickens were meant to do, using their sharp beaks to spear caterpillars, slugs, and all sorts of buggy goodness.

The fish-farming industry boasts that farmed salmon, one of the most popular species of farmed fish, has the lowest FCR of all, clocking in on a good day at about 1.2:1. However, farmed salmon, being carnivorous, are fed mainly fish meal and fish oil (i.e., ground-up smaller fish caught from already-diminishing wild populations and of species less popular among human consumers, like anchovies, sardines, and mackerel, all of which are high in fish oil). Essentially, farmed fish consume wild flesh protein and fat, and turn it into domesticated flesh protein and fat, meaning that their FCR can't really be fairly compared to that of grass-chewing cows. You'll pardon me if I'm not too impressed by their purported "efficiency." Taking one kind of animal protein and turning it into another is far less dramatic than transforming inedible landscape into hamburger.

The FCR of wild salmon is closer to that of cattle, around 10:1, largely because of the energy they spend catching all those smaller fish, none of which agreed to the deal.

Salmon are true carnivores, which means they cannot process carbohydrates from plants like the other animals mentioned can. Instead, they make their energy from fats like those in fish oil. That omega-3 we're all supposed to be getting more of in our diets? Salmon basically live off it. Like us, they can't make it themselves. Wild salmon get it from the smaller fish they eat, who get it either from krill or from microalgae. Farmed salmon get it by consuming 50 percent of the world's fish oil production.*

And finally, we get to bugs.

Crickets, like chickens, are omnivorous. They'll basically eat anything they can get their palpi on. Cornmeal, compost, cat food—all are fair fare for the cricket. They have a digestive system somewhat like a tiny chicken: Instead of a gizzard, they have a crop with hardened parts that act like teeth, grinding up their food. They also have a tiny cecum for fermentation. But the special thing that crickets, along with many other invertebrates (like termites, of course), produce is cellulase—that same enzyme the bacteria in a cow's rumen use to break down the fiber in plants. Until quite recently, it was thought that the production of cellulase was limited to plants, bacteria, and fungi, but many insect species have been found to carry it as well, both in their mouths and guts. For some evolutionary reason, only invertebrates produce this enzyme directly, but it certainly helps with their digestion of plants.

It's no surprise then that crickets have one of the lowest FCRs of the potential livestock kingdom, coming in somewhere between farmed fish and chickens, at about 1.5:1. This FCR comes from a highly vegetal diet. Crickets really can live, grow, and produce offspring on a mostly corn diet.

Precious little of a cricket, or a mealworm, or grasshopper, is wasted. Unlike the processing fish, chickens, pigs, and cows must undergo before their meat reaches the market, which vastly decreases their overall output volume, insects require

---

* According to the FAO website, 87 percent of the world's fish oil goes to aquaculture in general.

little to no deboning, gutting, plucking, or butchering. Insects, like oysters, are generally eaten whole. They also devote less food energy toward building things like bones, hooves, fur, and feathers, which we don't eat. While the throwaway portion of other animals can be up to 75 percent of their total weight, this is the same percentage of most insects that can be eaten.

Another reason crickets have such efficient FCRs is that unlike the majority of the other livestock animals, crickets, like all insects, are cold-blooded. This means that the food energy cows and pigs and chickens burn to keep their blood warm, crickets turn directly into body mass or offspring. It also means that crickets require a certain ambient temperature in order to reproduce quickly. Despite the fact that insects either need to be grown in warm climates or have a climate made artificially warm for them, energy sources like the sun for solar heating are far more sustainable and abundant than the use of land to grow massive amounts of food for warm-blooded livestock. Energy from the sun is infinite*; land space is finite.

Factors such as land space, water usage, and inhumane treatment are the real costs of raising animals like cows that — as your trip to McImpacts showed you — aren't always directly reflected in measurements like FCR or the commercial sticker price you see in the supermarket.

One cow requires anywhere from two to thirty acres. At the global level, raising cattle uses nearly a third of Earth's terrestrial surface not covered by ice, a fraction that's already huge and is constantly growing. Picture a giant cow taking

---

* Relatively speaking.

big bites out of the rain forest: 70 percent of formerly forested land in the Amazon is now used as pasture, while much of the rest is used for feed crops. In addition to the methane they produce by breaking down plant cellulose, the combination of cattle grazing and grain agriculture to feed cattle also destroys one of the main ways our planet handles excess CO_2: forests, which inhale CO_2 and exhale oxygen, the necessary opposite of what human lungs do. As forests are cut down to make room for not just cattle, but for the acres and acres of soy and corn to feed the cattle as well, Earth's lung capacity is steadily diminished. If you've ever seen an antismoking ad about emphysema, you know this is not a good thing.

The expansion of the cattle industry means that with one hand, we are destroying Earth's ability to process greenhouse gas–causing emissions, and with the other, we are adding even more GHGs to the mix. My favorite comedian, Maria Bamford, jokes, "Jesus turned the other cheek just to grab another can of whoop-ass." We're opening double cans of whoop-ass on our environment's capacity to balance our impact. Add in the emissions of cars and industry, and we might as well just smother it with a pillow.

And this is to say nothing of the incredible loss of biodiversity that goes along with the destruction of forest. Given how consistently researchers discover powerful new pharmaceutical compounds in exotic rain forest plants, we may have already sacrificed a cure for cancer for the sake of our Big Macs. Are our appetites worth life itself? Are we eating to live, or killing . . . everything?

As if that weren't enough to convince you to give eating insects a try, here are a few more factors in favor of bugs:

A cow gives birth to one calf per year. In that same time,

a pig can produce twenty-five to thirty piglets, and a chicken lays three hundred eggs. Salmon reproductivity can be highly variable, even in captivity, so let's stick to land animals for now.

In comparison to these warm-blooded livestock, a cricket lays around a hundred eggs in her three-month lifespan. Assuming half are male, that makes 50 female crickets, each laying a hundred eggs. After three months, we have 2,500 laying female crickets; in a year, 312,500,000. If 1,000 crickets weigh a pound, that's 312,500 pounds of cricket in a year, a weight equivalent to 312 cows. Even if only a tenth of the crickets survived, that's still equivalent to more than 30 cows.

Most farmable insects don't need the space that cows, pigs, chickens, or even fish do. Whereas cows need space to graze, chickens and pigs need room to forage, and fish need either roped-off sections of the ocean (with the risk of escape and potential contamination of wild populations) or pools of constantly purified water, insects like crickets and mealworms do just fine in small boxes. Crickets, though they have wings, rarely use them to fly and prefer to spend the majority of their energy walking around eating and mating. Just as most of us would rather live in a city and drive to the supermarket than run down a deer in the woods, crickets do not show signs of ill effects when living in close quarters with their food and brethren. If you've ever opened an old bag of flour and found mealworms wriggling around, you know that they are also perfectly happy to reside in small, dark, enclosed spaces. As Dana Goodyear wrote in her 2011 *New Yorker* article "Grub: Eating Bugs to Save the Planet": "[I]nsect husbandry is humane: bugs *like* teeming, and thrive in filthy, crowded conditions." I'm going to suggest her word "filthy" could mean the more biologically accurate "fecund."

Raising insects on a large scale is possible in almost any human environment, from farmland to urban buildings. Unlike many of the other forms of livestock, insects can be farmed vertically and within city limits, reducing travel time and gas usage. On a smaller scale, they can even be raised within the home. Talk about eating local.

We wouldn't need to discuss skyscraper bug farms if the situation on Earth had not become so dire. We can't all see it yet, but we are essentially huddled on a shrinking iceberg, which grows smaller with every lap of an acid tide.

The United Nations expects the world human population to exceed 9 billion people by 2050, thirty-six years from now. In order to keep up with this explosion of mouths to feed, more food will have to be produced over the next few decades than has been produced in the past ten thousand years combined. We're going to have to figure out how to produce 70 percent more food than we are currently, while simultaneously maintaining enough forestland to keep Earth on life support.

Every twelve years or so, for the last several decades, we've been adding approximately a billion new people to our planet. Currently, around 1 billion of the people on the planet are hungry. Since the 7 billionth person was just born, that means that 1 in 7 people do not get the bare minimum of calories they need to function properly, let alone thrive, grow, or progress economically. Taking on another 2 billion people will not shift the numbers any closer to balance; rather, it is likely that close to 3 out of 9 people, or roughly one-third of the globe, will experience the devastating effects of hunger.

In the '60s and '70s, when food shortages first reared their frightening heads, the agriculture industry in the developed world responded with the "Green Revolution," which vastly increased global food production through better farming practices, increased fertilization, and improved pest control. However, these strategies may have reached their limit. Chemical fertilizers, pesticides, and heavy irrigation have taken major environmental tolls. Our soil is tapped out, and our oceans and freshwater systems are polluted. Algal blooms, feeding on fertilizer runoff, stretch their arms across reefs, lakes, and riverbeds, blocking out the sun and sucking up the oxygen, suffocating native species. Farmed soil is drained of nutrients, which are replaced by industrial, often petroleum-derived supplements. Livestock waste ferments in carefully sealed pools; one leak and the local drinking water is toast. Rain forests are felled to make room for cattle grazing, or soybeans, which are industrially fertilized and fed to said cows to fatten them for market. The bronchioles of Earth's lungs are soldered off, the blood clogged with the saturated fat of civilization, the flesh sucked dry by 7 billion voracious vampires.

Despite the high ideals of movements like "slow food" and locavorism, the only currently known way to efficiently produce enough protein to feed Earth's growing population is to further intensify industrial farming practices. This means doubling down on the factory farming of animals, packing more bodies into smaller areas. This is not good news for cows, pigs, or other animals that need things like space and fresh air. It is, however, just fine for many species of insects. Bring on the cramped conditions, the darkness, the teeming populace.

We are running out of options and have exhausted our alternatives. We need an idea with legs. Insects have six of them.

2

The Real Paleo Diet

"HOLY SHIT! WORMS!"
The guy behind me has registered the chalk menu hanging on Don Bugito's booth at the Off the Grid pop-up food market. Don Bugito is the nation's first gourmet, edible insect street food purveyor.

For the occasion, food trucks and vinyl-awninged booths have circled their wagons at the Fort Mason Center, just beyond the clinking, creaking San Francisco marina with its boats that rise and fall as if breathing. It's nearing 10 P.M. on a Friday night in October, almost closing time for the last event of the year. The sky is black and the air is cold; it's the foodies' last chance to sit outside in clusters, watching sports on truck-mounted TVs, drinking beer and trading tastes inside one of the world's hippest gypsy food courts. The next Off the Grid event won't be until March.

I turn to the man and offer him a crisped wax moth larvae from my *tacos de gusanos*. He takes it, curious, and pops it into his mouth.

"Oh, it's actually pretty good," he tells his grimacing girl-friend, who backs away when I offer her a taste, too.

She pulls him onward, scowling at him incredulously, her disapproval palpable. I wonder if he's getting any tonight.

Monica Martinez and her crew are trying to sell off the ex-cess inventory by slashing prices. The Mexico City–style corn, in particular, has to go, she tells me, double-checking its tem-perature in an insulated cooler of hot, sugared water with a meat thermometer. The bugs will keep for a few weeks in the fridge and can be used at one of her other gigs. But the corn won't.

"I *hate* wasting food," she says.

Drawn in by the low, low prices, a Latino family orders several of the seasoned cobs to go. Alejandra, one of the crew members, hastily prepares them, quickly brushing on *mayonesa*, rolling them in *queso cotija*, and sprinkling on *chile con limón*.

"Con amor, con amor," Monica urges her, making a smoothing motion with her hand, a *maestra* instructing her pupil. Alejandra smiles, straightens up, and resumes sprin-kling at a more leisurely, artful pace. The cobs are then wrapped in tinfoil and handed to the happy family, who likely hasn't seen these since their last trip to Mexico.

"People love this corn," Monica tells me. "A food network show from London came to do a story on me, and all they cared about was the corn. They were like, 'Bugs, whatever.'"

Overlooking the bugs in this case would take some do-ing. Alongside a colorful row of Jarritos soda bottles (also a big seller), the main display is striking: two entrées, covered in insects. One is a blue corn taco with cheese, avocado, and cilantro topped with a mass of fried larvae, covered in a dark green chile sauce, and garnished with pink pickled onions. The other is a *tostada de grillos*, a crunchy tortilla topped with guacamole, sour cream, pine nuts, and toasted crickets.

Both are legitimately, objectively delicious. The larvae taco tastes, as agreed upon by several customers, like *chicharrónes,* or pork cracklings. The crickets on the tostada, especially taken in with the *piñones* (pine nuts), are like hollow, roasted pistachios or almonds.

Don Bugito began as an art project. A Rhode Island School of Design grad, Monica's artistic background shines through in her various exploits: an art installation called Wurm-Haus, a miniature, Bauhaus-inspired habitat for growing mealworms; the Don Bugito Prehispanic Snacke-ria, a street-food project serving native Mexican dishes featuring insects; and the high-end dinners she has put on with her husband, artist Phil Ross. There is a gourmet, primitive-meets-modern aesthetic sensibility to the dishes she serves at events, like at a recent dinner at the Headland Center for the Arts in Sausalito, California: *escamoles* (ant eggs) sautéed in brown butter with pasilla peppers and Mexican zucchini, topped with avocado and wrapped in handmade blue corn tortillas; delicate corn custard with spicy tomato sauce and crisped wax worms; Anahuac salad with toasted crickets, jicama, sweet potato, and toasted pumpkin seeds with pumpkin lime vinaigrette and pumpkin chips; crispy toffee mealworms served over vanilla ice cream, sprinkled with *alegría* (popped amaranth seeds), and drizzled with bright pink prickly pear syrup.

It's not hard to be seduced by Monica's edible art, itself a history lesson taken in through the taste buds. Nearly every ingredient dates back to early pre-Columbian cultures. Many ingredients we think of as staples of our own food culture in fact originated from this one part of the world, and Mexico in particular: vanilla, corn, squash and squash seeds, peppers, avocadoes, tomatoes, and even potatoes. Though we don't realize it, the truth is that most of the world eats "Mexican food" on a near-daily basis.

Both vanilla and chocolate were originally used by the Aztecs. The supply of genuine vanilla is limited because the vanilla orchid depends on its symbiotic relationship with a local species of stingless bee. Although synthetic vanilla is used constantly in food and fragrances, real vanilla is second only to saffron in expense.

Squash, beans, and corn were planted together because of their cooperative nature and were known as the Three Sisters. The corn provided a structure for the beans to climb, the beans provided nitrogen to the soil, and the squash provided ground cover, blocking sunlight to prevent the growth of weeds. Nutritionally, corn lacks the amino acids lysine and tryptophan, which the beans provide, creating whole protein. Squash seeds provide fat and protein, while squash flesh provides vitamins A and C.

Chili peppers are excellent appetite stimulants and also provide vitamins. The word "chili" in chili pepper comes from the Aztec Nahuatl word *chilli.*

The word "jicama" (a.k.a. Mexican turnip) comes from the Nahuatl *xicamatl* (pronounced *shi-ka-MAT-l*).

Prickly pears, known regionally as *tunas*, are seen on the Mexican coat of arms. In the first European report on them in 1526, Spanish state officer Gonzalo Fernández Oviedo y Valdéz wrote of this fruit "that turned the urine red, which aroused great fear and became a prank played on newcomers."

Tomatoes, too, were part of Mesoamerican cuisine as early as 500 BC and didn't make it to Italy until almost two thousand years later, after the Spanish conquest of Tenochtitlán. Even then, they were seen as ornamentals for many years before being finally, and famously, adopted into the culinary sphere.

The potato dates back even further, to around 5000 BC. After the Spaniards conquered the Inca empire, they brought the potato to Europe, where it soon became indispensable. In fact, the Irish potato famine was a result of lack of diversity in imported potato species. There are more than thirty-five hundred varieties of potato in Peru alone.

Many aspects of native Mesoamerican cuisine have clearly been popularized over the centuries. So why not insects?

Most of this edible history flies over the heads of those who eat Monica's food — but that doesn't make it any less delicious.

Next to her eye-catching food art, Monica herself is subtler, minimalistic almost. Her stark, Aztec-flavored beauty is unadorned, set off by jet-black hair and a sharp but muted fashion sense. She is straightforward, blunt even. She is a hardworking Mexican woman trying to make her way in this world like anyone else. She has chosen an unusual field.

The mental gong has sounded, so everyone begins packing up their booths, giving away the last bits of food to their buddies and neighbors. Monica hands over a wax worm taco to Keith, who's working the Belly Burgers booth next door.

"So these are mealworms?" Keith asks, pointing down at the taco. For the umpteenth time that night, Monica makes the correction: They are wax moth larvae. Keith fingers a hole in his shirt. "Oh, like *moths.*"

We laugh. "Not that kind. Wax moth larvae live in beehives."

Keith shrugs. Whatever. Bugs are bugs. With the rest of the Belly Burgers crew watching, he takes a big bite of his taco.

"Oh, that's actually good," he says, chewing.

"What do they taste like?" I press, tallying descriptions in my notebook.

"Like puffed rice."

"Really?" asks Aurelia, his blond, tattooed, dreadlocked coworker, jumping down from her perch across the booth. "I want to try."

He hands her a larva. I snap a picture of her holding it between two tattooed fingers—together, they read "Dreadzilla," her old Roller Derby name. She pops it in her mouth.

"Oh, that is effing *good*. I would totally eat that," she says, asking for another. Later she spies her friend Tina, a bartender, ordering a wax moth taco from Monica.

"Dude, the mealworms are frigging good," she yells.

"Wax moth larvae," Keith corrects.

"Wax moth larvae," says Aurelia.

Tina takes her taco and heads back to her booth. "YOLO," she says as she passes the Belly Burgers crew, biting into the taco.

These kids aren't your average food truck employees. They all wait tables or bartend at some of the most respected joints in town: Foreign Cinema, Beast and the Hare, Alembic Bar. They're all graduates of foodie college, picking up a few extra hours at the hip installation that is Off the Grid.

Still, despite their street cred, most of them have never seen anything like what Monica's doing. She's making food news out of food history.

You've probably heard of the Stone Age diet craze known as the Paleolithic Diet, made popular most recently by Dr. Loren Cordain's bestseller *The Paleo Diet*. The premise is simple: If our early human ancestors couldn't have eaten it, we shouldn't, either. It's the one time, it seems, that being like a caveman is a good thing.

The theory goes (and archaeological evidence corroborates) that early hunter-gatherers, while they may not have lived as long, still had some major health advantages on most of us modern humans. They were much taller, averaging six-foot-five to our five-foot-eleven; had stronger, heavier bones; had more robust immune systems; and were leaner, tougher, and hardier than we are today. Higher levels of physical activity also played a vital role in cave people's vitality, and so did their high levels of wild food consumption: wild game meat, gathered greens and fruits, and healthy fats such as nuts.

Dr. Cordain suggests that prior to the agricultural revolution, early humans ate this Paleo Diet for 2.5 million years. The ten thousand years since the popularization of farming—or just 333 human generations—he says, is clearly a drop in the chronological bucket when compared with the millennia leading up to it. Thus, he maintains, the hunter-gatherer diet our ancestors lived on is far more deeply and indelibly imprinted into our DNA than our habits of the last few thousand years. I'm inclined to agree with him. In fact, I'm going to see his 2.5 million years and raise him a few millennia, and show you what we were *really* designed to eat. The real Paleo Diet would have included bugs. Lots and lots of bugs.

Fifty million years ago, the initial specter of modern humanity's blueprint lay in the genes of a tiny, furry, wide-eyed, long-tailed creature called a tarsier,* one of the world's very

---

* "Their exact nature is controversial but the current consensus is that they were roughly similar to today's bush babies, dwarf lemurs, and tarsiers—small, active nonanthropoidal primates whose nutrition is largely dependent on insects and other small invertebrates." S. Boyd Eaton and Dorothy A. Nelson, "Calcium in Evolutionary Perspective," *American Journal of Clinical Nutrition* 54, no. 1 (1991): 281s-7s.

first primates. The tarsier was one of the first mammals to have opposable thumbs and enormous, forward-facing eyes, both characteristics vital to our later success as a species.

Guess what he ate?

That's right, the tarsier was an insectivore. Now, that doesn't mean he enjoyed the odd bug here and there with his dinner of leaves and fruit. It means he primarily ate insects. It was very nearly all bugs, all the time for our cute little pro-simian ancestor. Unless you're not getting the picture clearly enough: yes, one of our earliest incarnations as a species was an adorable fuzzy tree-dweller who simply loved stuffing him-self with every bug he could find. The Garden of Eden for our collective ancestor would have been the bug tunnel scene in *Indiana Jones and the Temple of Doom.*

"From the time mammals first appeared until 50 million years ago—a total of 150 million years, three quarters of the entire time mammals have existed—our ancestors were pri-marily insectivorous," write S. Boyd Eaton and Dorothy A. Nelson in their paper "Calcium in Evolutionary Perspective." "Given the slow and conservative nature of genetic evolution, this long-standing adaptation for insect consumption must have made a significant impact on our genetic heritage. Con-sequently, the nutritional properties of insects have relevance for understanding the forces that have shaped the nutritional requirements of present-day humans."

It's easy to observe this early pre-human diet in the wild today, since versions of this prehistoric bug-guzzler still ex-ist in the form of bush babies, tree shrews, and similar small mammals. It turns out that for a certain size of primate, bugs are one of the best things on the planetary menu. If we were still that size, that's pretty much all we'd eat, too.

But for whatever reason, we grew, in both body and brain

size. And as we grew, it became harder to find enough insects to fulfill our daily nutritional requirement. The problem was not with the bugs themselves, but just that *we couldn't find enough of them.* We had to start branching out. We had to find something more dependable as a source of calories than that which could see us coming and, say, crawl into a hole. So we started eating plants, which, of course, couldn't run away. This is one of the miracles and geniuses of being a primate: our innate adaptability to different diets, also known as omnivory ("omni" = everything, "vory" = eating). We adapted so that we could eat everything and anything and still survive.

We changed inside and out in order to take advantage of the different types of nutrient sources around us, and as we evolved, we took different paths to get there. Some primates adapted internal organs so that they could digest cellulose and extract protein and other nutrients from leaves like herbivores. Some grew long tails and relocated to the treetops, where the good fruit was, and lived off that. Meanwhile others—the ones who eventually became humanity—moved to the savanna, where they could see both prey and predators coming and still find enough vegetable matter to supplement their diets.

But the one thing that none of these versions of ourselves ever stopped eating, at least when they had the chance, was insects. From lemurs and other New World apes, up through Old World apes like chimpanzees and gorillas, up through prehominids, hominids, Neanderthals, and, finally, humans, one thing that unites primatehood throughout the ages is an enduring appetite for bugs.

The main reason for this is that insects are a much higher-quality food compared to things like leaves, fruits, flowers, and even nuts. Just like other animals, insects are a trophic level two food source—they themselves have eaten, and thereby concentrated in their own tissues, the nutrients found in plant sources, providing the sorts of things that primates thrive on: protein, iron, calcium, and, best of all, healthy, unsaturated long-chain essential fatty acids (EFAs).

Sure, these nutrients can be found in plant sources, too, but you have to eat *a lot more of them.* Insects are these scrumptious little compact packages of food that make surviving, and thriving so much easier for a foraging primate. Nutrition is sort of like money: If leaves represent dollar bills, fruits are fives, nuts are tens, and insects, and other forms of animal flesh, are crisp fifty-dollar bills. The nutrients in them are just more concentrated and often more bioavailable, which means the body has to do less work to utilize them.

At this point in the conversation, the inevitable question comes up: Why eat animals at all? Why not just eat more vegetables? Vegans are particularly vocal on this point, and many argue that there are plenty of existing, thriving primates who subsist on a fully vegan diet, with either zero or "insignificant" amounts of animal flesh. However, more recent studies have shown that most of these animals—at least the ones with digestive systems like ours—jump at the chance to eat insects, especially during seasonal upcroppings of caterpillars, ant colony invasions, or locust swarms. Although I have great respect for its practitioners, I fundamentally disagree with the concept of veganism. Veganism is a beautiful philosophy, and the idea of wanting to protect and respect one's fellow earthlings is commendable. Including more fruits and veggies in a diet is inarguably a good idea, and the attention vegans have brought to the poor treatment of farm animals and our existing primate cousins' diets is important.

But veganism is ultimately just that, a philosophy. And

there simply isn't any evidence, archaeologically, historically, or physically, that supports it. If humans were designed to be vegan, it's very likely that we would never have *been* at all.

Let's examine the vegan philosophy for a moment. Many vegans have long based their diet on that of our primate cousins, namely chimpanzees, who share 90 percent of their DNA with humans and were thought, for many years, to eat an almost completely vegan diet. This hypothesis was accepted for a while until it was discovered that not only do chimps eat insects like crazy but that they also hunt small game, including monkeys. Once chimps were out, these vegans had to find another primate champion for their ideals. Gorillas share only slightly less DNA with humans, and look at them—they're huge! If they can support all that body mass on a vegan diet, then the average 150-pound human weakling should be able to do the same, right?

Wrong again. First of all, post-1960s research found that lowland gorillas also eat as many insects as are available to them, along with their fruits and leaves. Koko, the world's best-known lowland gorilla, who knows more than a thousand words in sign language, is fed animal protein on a regular basis, and has a team of humans preparing her daily browse. What about mountain gorillas? They live in a cold climate, eat mostly leaves, and weigh half a ton. If they can do it, surely, with a little discipline and a lot of doctrine, so can we, right?

Well, we could *if* we had their digestive prowess (and flexible schedules). Compare the relative sizes of the digestive organs of various primates, and you'll see how the gorilla's stomach and colon are much bigger, while the human small intestine (usually used for high-protein processing) is three times longer than any other ape's.

Highland gorillas are built big for a reason: to house their monster digestive systems. Gorillas have stomachs and colons that are twice the size of ours. In a great ape chicken-and-egg mystery, their physical largeness is both a result of their diet as well as the cause. Gorillas had to get big in order to house the organs necessary to synthesize the nutrients they need from the food they eat. Remember the giant cow rumens? Gorillas have digestive systems that perform similar functions and the giant torsos to hold them.

Mountain gorillas spend the day stuffing their big stomachs with mostly leaves—up to 40 pounds a day—as well as some fruit, some flowers, and, incidentally, the small bugs and grubs curled up inside of said plant matter—a food source that zookeepers have found they have to replace with small servings of meat in captivity or else the apes become weak. Fruit, flowers, and bugs, again, are nice food if you can get 'em, but the bread and butter of the mountain gorilla's diet is leaves, up to 85 percent of their calories. These leaves are passed into their giant colons, where special bacteria, similar to those in a cow's intestine, break down the cellulose and unlock the plants' nutrients. A gorilla actually gets more protein, energy, and overall sustenance out of the plants that it eats than a human ever could, no matter how desperately a human wants to.

Here's the other great thing about leaves for gorillas—in addition to being plentiful, they're inert, so the gorilla doesn't have to put out a lot of energy to collect them. This is a good thing, since the gorilla doesn't have a lot of energy to spare. The image of the peaceful gorilla is largely due to chemistry. They simply don't have the calories to waste on a lot of activity. Their whole econiche lifestyle only works if they stay within certain energetic, caloric, and habitat-related grounds.

They spend their whole day eating lots of a low-quality food (remember those dollar bills?), digesting it with special equipment, and not moving much so as not to overspend their energy.

If you were to live and eat like a gorilla, instead of taking short breaks throughout the day to eat, you'd spend your whole day eating while taking short breaks to do other things. You'd sleep a lot—about thirteen hours a night, as well as several siestas throughout the day. Harley Johnstone, cofounder of 30 Bananas a Day, an online forum and one of the world's most popular vegan websites, says he sleeps eleven to twelve hours a night and isn't ashamed of it. Let me tell you, I'm a big sleeper and rester—as Maria Bamford said, "I'd live up to my potential, but it would really cut into my sitting-around time"—but even I would have trouble fitting this into my life.

If you lived and ate like a gorilla, you'd never get anything done and would have difficulty holding down a job or even a hobby. Gorillas, luckily, aren't expected to. When given the opportunity to gather up a bunch of bugs without exerting too much energy—for example, when ant colonies swarm—mountain gorillas, those revered vegetarians, go bananas for them. They beat their chests in excitement and eat as many as possible because ants are a very high-quality food source.

Some primatologists suggest that when seeking evidence for primitive dietary habits, instead of looking at our primate cousins from a phenotypical or DNA-sharing standpoint, we should instead be comparing digestive systems. From this perspective, our closest relative is the savanna baboon.

Wait a second, you're saying. Baboons? Has it really come to this? Bear with me. If there's any ape we should be comparing ourselves to, diet-wise, it turns out that savanna baboons hit the nail pretty much on the stomach. Theirs is the closest to our own digestive layout: similar relative stomach capacity, colon length, and, most of all, small intestine.

Still don't believe me? Take a look at your front yard, and if you don't have one, picture the American dream. You know, the one with the white picket fence. What does it fence in? A green lawn, probably offset with some trees, bushes, a few flowers . . . in other words, a suburban savanna. Studies have shown that humans tend to gravitate toward these green expanses, punctuated by a few trees, even on a global level. See: Japanese, French, and English gardens.

Savanna baboons live pretty much the way our early human ancestors did. During much of the year, they eat grasses, fruits, tubers, and small vertebrates. But wait until caterpillar or termite season. They spend 70 percent of their time and energy chasing after this particular high-quality food. Think Homer Simpson while the McRib is available.

Now that we've compared digestive anatomy, it's time to take a look at another aspect of primatehood: our disproportionately large brains. A ratio system called the encephalization quotient (EQ) is used to roughly measure the intelligence of a species. The EQ essentially uses the mass of the animal's body to predict the mass of its brain. Using this ratio system, human brains are found to be at least seven times larger than expected. Based on the statistics of the rest of the animal kingdom, our body mass should indicate a much smaller brain. Instead, we have, by far, the largest EQ on the planet: 7.5. This means that our brains are at least seven times larger than they should be, considering our body mass. Bottlenose dolphins are a distant second, with an EQ of 4, and chimpanzees come in at about 2.5.

Human brains, in addition to being incongruously large, also take up a huge amount of energy. In their paper *Ecology and Energetics of Encephalization in Hominid Evolution,* biological anthropologists R. A. Foley and P. C. Lee found that the overall energetic maintenance costs of the human brain are about three times that of a chimpanzee. Our brains suck up 20–25 percent of the energy we eat, compared with the average ape-brain usage of 8 percent. While the rest of the primate world is puttering around in cerebral Priuses, we're revving Porsches. And like most sports cars (Teslas excluded), they require more fuel of a higher grade in order to run properly.

The developing human brain depends on long-chain essential fatty acids (EFAs): the omegas-3, -6, and -9. The Paleo Diet philosophy is partly based on the assumption that omega fatty acid intake was higher in a wild, hunter-gatherer diet and may have contributed to better overall health. After brain development, EFA intake remains important for maintaining healthy brain and nerve function, cell development, and regulating proper thyroid and adrenal activity. EFAs also help lower inflammation, protect against heart disease, and can even help inhibit tumor formation.

We can get EFAs from some plants, seeds, and nuts, but the quality and quantity of it tends to be best and most bioavailable when it comes from animals like fatty ocean fish and shellfish. Humans, many other mammals, as well as these fish have to ingest EFAs from their diets, because they can't synthesize or create them internally. Plants, algae, and many insects can.

Aquatic insects, like the kind young Atlantic salmon subsist on during their initial freshwater phase, are particularly high in EFAs. Crickets and cockroaches have both been found to synthesize linoleic acid (LA), an omega-6 fatty acid.

Termites, in particular, are an excellent source of long-chain fatty acids. They are such a good source of these brain-building nutrients that there's a theory that they may have been one of the ways our brains were able to grow in the first place—because we had a steady source of long-chain fatty acids, ideal for building brain tissue.

Another theory suggests that we originally received these essential fats from seafood, which makes a great deal of sense. When early prehominids discovered shellfish and other ocean and freshwater life, they hit the jackpot of abundant protein and fats with virtually no competition for its calories. It would be like if you discovered an alternate Apple or Microsoft that no one else was investing in. You'd skyrocket ahead of everyone else. And skyrocket we did, developmentally.

Let's stick with the termites for the time being because they are an excellent alternate source of these fatty acids. They are like the HP version of protein—less expensive and more widely accessible. Termites can also be found at the scene of many primate developmental milestones, such as tools.

When you think of the hallmarks of evolution, what image pops up? For many, it's the picture of a chimp with a stick, moistened to catch termites. But like a dog that stares at the pointing finger instead of the ball, we've been focusing entirely on the tool and ignoring its ultimate purpose: to capture and consume insects more efficiently. Scientists in the Congo River Basin have observed chimps utilizing a collection of implements, a "toolkit" if you will, in order to better harvest termites: one short stick to puncture an aboveground mound, and then a longer, slenderer "fishing probe" to pull the termites out. This fishing probe was often further modified to increase its effectiveness. The chimps used their teeth to fray the end like a paintbrush, the better to collect the insects with.

Infant chimps watch carefully as their mothers collect and customize stick tools, find and puncture termite mounds, and deftly extract the crawling black morsels. It is this process of watching, learning, and assimilating through social interaction and observed behavior that many scientists believe to be the roots of civilization.

In fact, as it turns out, the skill of collecting termites is easier observed than done. In a tertiary cultural exchange when the scientists themselves tried to extract termites from the mounds using the same tools and methods the chimps did, they found it quite difficult. "We were less successful than most of the [chimp] youngsters—this is a complex skill that is developed with years of practice," said the appropriately named coauthoring anthropologist Crickette Sanz.

Humanity's great technological and cultural achievements likely began in much the same way. The earliest bone tools found by archaeologists are thought to have been used specifically for insect gathering. A 2001 study on bone tools left behind by *Australopithecus robustus,* a million-plus-year-old distant relative to modern humans, theorized that they were used to scrape away at termite mounds in order to harvest the inhabitants. This was the first evidence that our early human ancestors were "methodical insectivores."

And it's no wonder, according to paleontologist Dr. Lucinda Backwell, who coauthored the study, since termites have a higher nutritional content than rump steak.

"Termites are a valuable source of protein, fat and essential amino acids, in the diets of both primates and modern humans," wrote Dr. Backwell with her partner, Francesco d'Errico. "While rump steak yields 322 calories per 100 grams, and cod fish 74, termites provide 560 calories per 100 grams."

Let's imagine you are an evolving protohuman, and you have this excellent source of protein, fat, and other nutrients, and it doesn't require you to run, throw a spear, or hold your breath. Insect eating, during the right seasons, is like the drive-through window at McDonald's—a big caloric payoff for comparatively low energetic output.

Dr. Cordain and other Paleo Diet advocates and researchers paint a picture of early man as an aggressive and skillful hunter, bringing home piles of meat to his hungry family. But reality was likely quite different. And here is the bug in the system, or, rather, the glaring lack thereof.

As the author of the blog *PaleoVeganology* quips, "It's as though someone took a big can of Raid to the authors' paleo-imaginations. So steeped are they in their Western food bias and paleofantasies that the possibility of Paleolithic man fulfilling his nutrient requirements with a diet of creepy-crawlies never occurred to them."

Hunting, especially in the Neolithic age, was quite a risky activity, both from a safety and energy investment standpoint. Twisting an ankle in the bush or being injured by a charging animal without any medical care could mean death. It was also a very hit-or-miss sort of activity. Even today's hunters with their semiautomatic weapons, laser sights, GPSs, cell phones, and off-road vehicles, do not experience 100 percent success rates. Imagine how much more difficult it was with just a spear.

Early hunters experienced about a 20 percent success rate. That means two to three out of every ten times they ventured out they *might* return with a big dead animal. Granted, some of these kills would feed the tribe for several days or even weeks, but at those rates, they would have starved if not for the steady stream of calories brought in by gathered and foraged food, such as tubers, greens, and small animals that included, to a large extent, insects and other invertebrates. On a day-to-day basis, things like insects would have been regular fare, the kinds of things that kept early people going between big kills.

In order to do this type of gathering, though, an animal had to be able to hold things in its hands and still travel. It had to be able to walk upright—you try walking on all fours while holding something in your hands. If you look at it that way, it's even been suggested that the gathering of things like insects would have influenced our shift to bipedalism. Yes, you could, if you wanted to, even partially credit bugs with your ability to *walk*.

Since it was usually the men doing the hunting (this is the case even in chimpanzee communities), the women would have been the ones gathering, as it's something that can be done with a baby on your back. While the men went out and often came back empty-handed, the women came home every day with at least something to feed the tribe, their mates, and, most important, their children. The majority of the day-to-day protein was actually provided by women and, potentially, largely through insects.

Despite the fact that women were providing a daily stream of protein, insects were less valued culturally, of course, than the giant mammoth kill that fed the whole tribe for a month and got all the hunters laid like crazy. Seriously, coming in from the bush dragging a giant dead animal made you the caveman version of Jon Bon Jovi crossed with Bear Grylls— rock star, killer, provider. Those cavewomen couldn't get their leather panties off fast enough, even while their own daily drudgery was overlooked as less culturally valuable. As anthropologist and author Marvin Harris wrote, a big kill would have people talking about it around the fire for a year, even while they ate their grubs and whatever else their womenfolk brought in from that day's foraging.

A four-year study on savanna chimpanzees, conducted by anthropologists Jill Pruetz and Paco Bertolani, yielded the observation that it is the female chimps, by and large, who use tools to hunt, not the males.

"In the chimp literature, there is a lot of discussion about hunting by adult males, because basically, they're the only ones that do it—and they don't use tools," said Pruetz. "Females are rarely involved. And so this was just kind of astounding on a number of different levels. It's not only chimps hunting with tools, but females . . ."

Pruetz and Bertolani concluded that this discovery supports a theory that females played a significant role in the evolution of tool technology among the earliest humans.

Oh, how times have changed: When an early female hominid saw a bug and shrieked, it was in excitement, because hey, lunch.

We highfalutin modern humans may have a hard time believing it, but our evolution has always been intertwined with the eating of bugs. We began eating bugs, and they sustained us throughout our development. They are inextricable from our modern food systems, and when we die, they eat us. Instead of "from dust to dust," it is perhaps somewhat more immediately accurate to say "from bugs to bugs."

Take a moment and look down at yourself. Every cell in your body may have once come from an insect of some kind, somewhere along the evolutionary pathway. Your ancestors ate them; your global neighbors eat them; you eat them by accident on a near-daily basis. So why fight it? After all, it's so easy a caveman could do it. Just add a little chocolate or chili, and you've got a Paleo snack that's as old as time itself.

3

Why Eat Bugs?

We should all be eating insects. And we all will be eating insects. They're a perfectly reasonable source of protein.

—RUTH REICHL

PATRICK CROWLEY IS passionate about water. True to his passion, Pat is a consultant at SWCA Environmental Consultants in Salt Lake City, Utah. Water availability, like food production, is one of the major issues facing the globe in the next fifty years, so he's always thinking about creative solutions to this problem.

One day on his commute into town he was listening to a TED Talk by Dr. Marcel Dicke* on the sustainability of edible insects as food when a lightbulb went on in his head. Why not eat bugs? That's when he came up with the idea for Chapul, the world's first cricket-based energy bar company. Chapul means "cricket" in Nahuatl.

Pat had been focused on water conservation long before

---

* Pronounced DEE-kah.

he started making cricket bars. As a National Outdoor Leadership School instructor, he led rafting trips down the Grand Canyon, where he'd first become acquainted with water issues in the western United States.

"We don't really have a plan for where our water's going to come from in the future," Pat says. "On the long-term graphs, there are these big bars of 'Future Water Resources.' No one really knows what they are, it's not defined. We're just kind of relying on future generations to come up with something. I thought, 'We're the ones supposed to be figuring this out.'"

As we sit down to a meal at a Himalayan restaurant, Pat tells me about the time he led a rafting trip down the Ganges, which brought his awareness of the global water problem to a head. He explains that the Himalayan glacial field is the fastest-receding glacier field in the entire world. Part of China and all of the Ganges River Basin rely on the ice melt for water, especially during periods of drought. Some people, he says, predict that it's a matter of a decade or two until it's totally gone—the water supply for 1.8 billion people. The people there are much closer to issues that we'll face soon, too, if we continue mining a diminishing resource like water, our demand for which is ever increasing.

"We're not going to face that in the next decade or two, but in fifty or a hundred years from now, absolutely, if we continue on this trajectory. We have to do something about it, or we'll be *forced* to do something about it."

So what do water and glacial fields have to do with, well, crickets?

In the West, 80 percent of our water goes to agriculture, including both plant crops and livestock. Meanwhile, a lot of the money we spend on water conservation goes to the domestic sector, which is a much smaller fraction of the pie chart compared with agricultural use. Only about 15 percent of America's water supply goes to domestic households, so turning the water off when you're brushing your teeth is a tiny drop in the overall bucket of water conservation.

"The real beast in the room is agricultural water use," says Pat. Listening to Marcel Dicke's TED Talk made him realize that the key to water conservation is actually agriculture.

Of the 80 percent of water that's used for agriculture, about half of it goes to growing feed for livestock. That 40 percent is the biggest single chunk of our water resources; water to grow food for cows and pigs far outstrips any other single usage. If we could cut down even a fraction of the agricultural use of water, Pat thinks, we would save more water than by any other measures we're currently taking.

Pat takes a sip of his water and realizes something—it's exactly a year to the day since he left for India to lead that rafting trip down the Ganges.

"Good ol' cosmos," he says, as if he were giving his close buddy Karma a noogie.

Confluence seems to have a lot to do with Chapul's existence.

Two hundred years ago in this same part of the country, the Northern Ute Tribe traded "desert fruitcake," a cake made of ground, dried grasshoppers mixed with serviceberries, with the early settlers for goods. This type of cake, also known as pemmican, was the original energy bar—a portable, nutritious food that could be easily carried along and eaten during a hunt or trek.

Initially rejected by the European Americans, these bars later came to be appreciated. As journalist Edwin Bryant noted in 1849, after buying one Great Basin group out of its stock of bars, "The prejudice against the grasshopper 'fruitcake' was strong at first, but it soon wore off and none of the delicacy was thrown away or lost."

In his article "A Grasshopper in Every Pot: In the Desert West, Small Game Made Big Sense," archaeologist David Madsen writes of an unexpected discovery he made in 1984 in Lakeside Cave on the western edge of the Great Salt Lake. While digging into the deposits left by prehistoric Great Basin hunter-gatherers, he wrote, "[W]e found tens of thousands of grasshopper fragments. Bits of the insects pervaded every stratum we uncovered, and extrapolating to the entire floor area, we estimated that the cave contained remains from as many as five million hoppers."

At first, the explorers could think of no reason for the phenomenon, or why the grasshoppers were evenly layered with sand. Then they found remains of human feces near the site, which were chock-full of guess what? Grasshopper parts. The cave had served, probably for hundreds if not thousands of years, as a kind of climate-controlled pantry for dried bug goods.

As for the sand, not long after this initial discovery, an amateur archaeological team found something else: thousands of dried grasshoppers lying along the eastern shore of the lake.

"When we went to investigate, we found that enormous numbers of the insects had flown or been blown into the salt water and had subsequently washed up, leaving neat rows of salted and sun-dried grasshoppers stretched for miles along the beach," wrote Madsen.

As a result of varying wave action, as many as five separate rows of grasshoppers existed in places ranging from an inch to six feet wide and containing anywhere from five hundred to ten thousand grasshoppers per foot. The grasshoppers flew or were blown into the water by the thousands, where as they drowned, they were simultaneously pickled and dried. The researchers realized that instead of being a tedious gathering task, the foragers could have simply scooped up and consumed the "sun-dried product" directly, preserved as it was with salt and heat.

In areas without the benefit of saltwater lakes, other preservative and cooking methods were used by native people. At the beginning and end of the summer, grasshoppers and Mormon crickets (so named for the threat they posed to the Mormon's first crops in the mid-1800s) were driven into pits, where they were "roasted in trays like seeds and ground into meal and eaten as mush or cakes. . . . [T]hese insects are considered very great delicacies," wrote geologist and ethnologist John Wesley Powell in the 1870s.

Participants in the Lakeside Cave project who elected to try eating the dried grasshoppers themselves began referring to them as "desert lobster."

Madsen posited that eating these grasshoppers made excellent economical and nutritional sense. Calorically speaking, "One person collecting insects from the water margin for one hour, yielding eighteen and one-half pounds, therefore accomplishes as much as one collecting 87 chili dogs, 49 slices of pizza, or 43 Big Macs."

With the amount of pesticides used today, it is far less likely that such hordes of insects might be found in any one site as they were hundreds of years ago. Has the extermination of this source of food been worth it? Are the crops we save from locusts as nutritious as the locusts themselves?

The next morning after my dinner with Pat, I leave my rental car at the hotel and walk the mile across Salt Lake City to get to Artspace Commons, a LEED Gold–certified community plaza where Chapul rents commercial kitchen space three days a week. Walking in Salt Lake is like traversing a giant fishbowl: flat on the bottom, with red mountains that seem to rise straight up from the edge of town.

A giant solar pyramid spikes up out of the Commons parking lot, a shining mirrored blade slicing between blue sky and red mountains. Photovoltaic awnings jut out above the windows in the concrete complex, providing shade as they drink in the sun. Pat waves me inside, wearing a brown Chapul T-shirt, big red-framed glasses, and gloves. The cooking space is stark and modern, yet artfully organic, kind of like a Whole Foods supermarket aesthetic. Floor-to-ceiling windows let in loads of natural light, except for one tall pane covered in a bamboo beaded curtain with Lakshmi, the Hindu goddess of abundance, painted on it. Standing in front of a line of solar ovens, Pat and Jai, a friend from Pat's capoeira classes and a Chapul coworker, are measuring out ingredients for the bars.

A lot of folks on the Chapul crew come from the capoeira classes Pat takes three times a week. Capoeira is a Brazilian martial art originally developed as a way for slaves to train in secret; if one of their Portuguese oppressors ever caught them at it, they claimed they were dancing. Remarkable for its many upside-down cartwheel and handstand-like moves, it is also known as the "drunken monkey dance" and includes elements of music, rhythm, and singing. Capoeira is now popular in cosmopolitan cities all over the world. Pat's group seems to have a bit of a church-like aspect to it, in that members help each other out with whatever's going on at the time, be it illness, financial problems, or starting a cricket protein bar company.

"Put the peanuts in first," Pat instructs Jai, who is dark and muscular and also wearing a Chapul shirt, which I am seriously beginning to covet. Jai sings a Brazilian song as he works, grinding peanuts and dried crickets, pouring agave syrup, and sifting cricket flour. Pat shows me how the larger bits of bug stay behind in the sifter: shreds of wings, hind legs, and fragments of exoskeleton. There's nothing wrong with them nutritionally, but they would affect the smooth texture of the bars.

A mixing machine whirs as it homogenizes the ingredients for Chaco bars, Chapul's Aztec-inspired bar. Chocolate is included, because cacao was favored by the early Aztecs, as well as peanuts, also eaten by pre-Hispanic cultures.* I tell them about how the agave plant, the source of tequila, was represented by the Aztec fertility goddess Mayahuel, who nursed her children, the Centzon Totochtin ("four hundred rabbits"), with her four hundred breasts. The Centzon Totochtin became the Aztec gods of drunkenness. Pat and Jai laugh, blushing.

Once the ingredients are mixed, Jai pours everything out onto a baking pan and presses it down with his gloved fingers into the corners of a metal frame—what Pat calls a "Chapul fence"—which creates a uniform edge for the bars. Pat says he had the fence made by a local welder just for this purpose.

He then rolls the "dough" out flat and slides it in the oven, and once it's baked, he uses a large metal baker's knife to cut it into rectangles. The rectangles are then slid into packages, slapped with Chapul stickers, and packed into boxes. A fairly simple, straightforward procedure.

While they work, a few more capoeira friends and co-workers stop by. At one point, Jai, Pat, and Aaron, Chapul's graphic designer, and Pat's girlfriend, Erica, are all in the kitchen at once, assembly-lining the bars and moving grace-

---

* Some people think they even invented peanut butter, well before George Washington Carver ate his first peanut.

fully around one another, like a slow dance, as they likely have learned to do in class. Jai begins singing that song again, and I jokingly suggest that the others back him up. They burst into sudden, startling harmony—another carryover from capoeira.

I stand there, agape, until they all start laughing, breaking the moment that had hovered as ephemerally as a rainbow on a soap bubble. It's hard not to feel just a little enchanted. So far, Chapul is not like any other start-up I've encountered.

It's been a good day—in the five or so hours we've been here, they've made 220 bars, which will sell at $2.50 apiece. Not a bad day's work for just a few people in a kitchen.

"It's still early days," says Pat, a humble statement in light of the fact that the company has already filled orders in thirteen countries since the cricket bars first debuted at the Twenty-Fifth Annual Bug Fair at the Los Angeles Natural History Museum in May 2012. The bar is now available in seventy-five stores across the United States, and the company expects sales to top $1 million next year.

A few years ago I gave a talk on insect nutrition to the International Society of Sports Nutrition in Las Vegas. Of all the audiences I've ever spoken to, they were the most enthusiastic about edible insects. So many of them came up to me after my speech that the next speaker began to get a little glare-y. My pockets overflowed with business cards. They all wanted me to alert them the moment an insect protein product of some kind went on the market. Used to a larger degree of skepticism, I remarked on their outpouring of excitement.

"Well," joked one of the attendees drily, "if you tell a bodybuilder that eating manure will help him put on muscle, he'll go out into a pasture with a fork."

Bodybuilders and extreme athletes tend to be early adopters of nutrition trends. That's why they are precisely the demographic Dianne Guilfoyle, a school nutrition supervisor in Southern California, hopes to capture with BugMuscle, a protein powder made up entirely of ground insects.

"If people see bodybuilders taking it, they might accept it more willingly," says Dianne, whose son Daniel is a cage fighter.

There are many benefits to using insects as a base for protein powder. For one, the main existing sources are soybeans and milk whey, both of which cause health concerns for some people.

Soy has long been touted as a meat alternative. For many years, soy products and isolated soy protein have been advocated by US doctors, nutritionists, and even the FDA. Studies showed that in certain Asian countries, like Japan and China, incidences of breast and prostate cancer were lower than in the United States, attributing this trend to common aspects of their traditional diets, such as soy products. However, the majority of these soy products bear a big contrast to their American counterparts: They are generally fermented. Foods like miso, *natto*, soy sauce, and fermented tofu are eaten frequently, but in moderation. The fact that they are consumed with lean protein, like fish, as well as seaweed and other vegetables, probably doesn't hurt, either.

Here in the United States, many doctors and industry professionals just saw the word "soy" and, with the typical Western attitude of "more is better," began applying it to foods across the board. Just as a pharmaceutical scientist might isolate the medicinally active part of plants to make pills, we isolated the protein from soybeans to make a concentrated protein powder.

In order to isolate the protein, and to "wash" the oil from

the beans, they are rolled into flakes and then soaked in a bath of hexane, a highly toxic solvent that is a major component of gasoline. Hexane is a potent neurotoxin, but the majority of it evaporates, leaving only a few, FDA-approved parts per million behind as a residue. My point here is not that eating soy protein powder is going to poison your brain, but rather that the process of obtaining and concentrating this supplement is not something that would likely be found in nature.

"The manufacture of soy protein isolate has always been a complicated, high-tech procedure," says Dr. Kaayla Daniel in her book *The Whole Soy Story: The Dark Side of America's Favorite Health Food.* "There's nothing natural about it—it takes place in factories, not kitchens."

It's not surprising, then, that we've run into some potential problems with it as a food source for humans.

Even unprocessed soy can have detrimental health effects. In a 2007 article for the *Utne Reader* entitled "The Dark Side of Soy," nutrition consultant Mary Vance wrote that for thirteen years, she thought she was maintaining a healthy vegetarian diet by frequently including soy products from beans to chik'n patties.

"After years of consuming various forms of soy nearly every day, I felt reasonably fit, but somewhere along the line I'd stopped menstruating," she wrote. "I couldn't figure out why my stomach became so upset after I ate edamame or why I was often moody and bloated. It didn't occur to me at the time to question soy, heart protector and miracle food."

Unfermented soy products contain phytic acid, which interferes with the body's absorption of certain minerals and nutrients, such as iron and zinc. Soy, like many plants, contains phytoestrogens: "phyto" for plant, and "estrogen" as in the hormone that stimulates fertility in female mammals. Phytoestrogens mimic our own estrogenic hormones, thus increasing the amount of them in our systems. Too much estrogen, however, is not a good thing and can contribute to breast cancer in women. Too much estrogen in the body of male mammals can contribute to decreased testosterone and, therefore, lowered reproductive potency.

Daniel notes in *The Whole Soy Story* that this might be why tofu was so readily adopted in early Chinese monasteries as a low-cost, vegetarian protein source.

"Over time, the monks may have noticed that randy behavior declined when tofu consumption went up. The aptly named 'meat without a bone' soon appeared regularly on monastery menus as an aid to spiritual development and sexual abstinence, a dietary strategy validated by recent studies showing that phytoestrogens in soy can lower testosterone levels."

In fact, this may be the very reason phytoestrogens exist: to decrease the reproductivity of male herbivores. Think about it. If a plant doesn't want to be eaten, and can't run away, all the better for it to produce a chemical that inhibits the desire of male herbivores to procreate. Less procreation, fewer offspring, and fewer mouths to feed on the plant's leaves come springtime.

Naturally, as mammals who depend on a certain endocrine balance, we wouldn't want to concentrate this hormone in our own systems if we can help it.

The other commonly used protein source for protein powders is whey. Whey is derived from dairy, so lactose allergies and concerns with the dairy industry can also be an issue. Whey is a by-product of cheese, yogurt, and other dairy man-

ufacturing; the cheese industry is the largest consumer of fac-
tory-farmed dairy. Long-term consumption of whey can tax
and even damage the liver and kidneys.

No single protein source is perfect (though for my money,
the less processed, the better).

While insect protein might not be a perfect alternative for
those with shellfish allergies, for others it could present an alternative that's healthier for their bodies and the planet than
some of the existing options. Previously, whey protein was the
only protein powder source to supply a complete amino acid
profile: all nine of the essential amino acids required for human nutrition. But guess what else is a great source of these
amino acids? That's right, insects.

Whey in its natural liquid form is only about 1 percent
protein by weight, whereas dried whey is 12 percent protein.
Processed whey protein isolate, marketed as the main ingredient in protein powder, is about 80 percent protein by
weight. In comparison, dried beef is about 50 percent protein.
Dried crickets weigh in at 65 percent protein. That's in their
whole, natural form, without industrial processing, unlike the
whey protein isolate. Cricket protein isolate doesn't exist yet,
though it has been proposed.

Clearly, we're looking at an interesting possibility here,
limited largely by lack of both research and public interest in
edible insects.

In addition to being high in protein, many edible insect species are also high in essential fatty acids, particularly
omega-3s. While fish remain one of the best, most concentrated natural sources of this important nutrient, you may
feel less comfortable eating fish when you learn how they are
sourced.

Farming salmon, for instance, brings with it a plethora of

problems, such as polychlorinated biphenyl (PCB) contamination and the use of pesticides to ward off sea lice (the pesticides and sea lice both drift into wild salmon populations), along with the use of antibiotics to keep the fish relatively healthy in cramped conditions. Many people are concerned about the idea that farmed salmon flesh is artificially colored. On the one hand, it is, and on the other, maybe this one aspect of fish farming isn't such a big deal, so let's get it out of the way first.

Without artificially added coloring, farmed salmon would indeed have very unappetizing-looking gray flesh and would probably not sell very well. Wild salmon have pink flesh because they absorb it from the krill they eat, which contain a red-pigmented phytochemical called astaxanthin. The same goes for flamingos, which would just be white without their diet of krill (and probably not nearly as popular as lawn ornaments). Astaxanthin is a carotenoid, like the one that makes carrots look orange. Interestingly, astaxanthin is the same pigment that turned those *chapulines* I ate in Mexico red, the same pigment that turns even blue lobsters and shrimp red when you cook them. Some nutritionists recommend astaxanthin as a powerful antioxidant, and in fact you can buy it as a nutritional supplement.

At any rate, the farmed salmon don't get enough, if any, krill in their diets to dye their naturally gray flesh a more appealing "salmon" pink, so the color has to be added in artificially or else consumers won't buy it. Fortunately, most salmon farmers tend to use astaxanthin supplements in their fish feed, which turns the farmed fishes' flesh the preferred pink. Although this difference between farmed and wild salmon seems the most obvious, it may not have a significant health impact.

The main health issue with farmed salmon is something you can't see, the potential concentration of toxins like PCB in their fatty tissues. PCBs are highly stable, toxic, viscous liquids that, among other applications, were used for decades* to insulate and cool electrical equipment, before being largely banned in 1979. Their stability was part of their success as an industrial chemical, and it is now part of the environmental problem. They don't easily break down in natural environments, like water, but are highly soluble in fats and oils, and can even penetrate skin. This means that they will remain intact in seawater, where they tend to accumulate, but absorb quite well into the fatty tissues of animals *in* the water, like salmon. This is why some experts suggest removing the skin and fat from the salmon you eat, to minimize your intake of possible PCBs. PCB intake has been linked with a host of health problems, including cancer.

As you may recall, farmed salmon are fed a combination of mashed-up smaller fish, like sardines, and fish oil. The fish oil is extracted and concentrated from millions of fish from all over the world. Since farmed salmon burn far less fat "catching" their food pellets than their wild brethren do pursuing live prey, they tend to have fattier tissues and, thus, more potential PCBs. Personally, I actually like the taste of a nice fatty salmon, but not when I think about what's in that fat.

Mercury, by the way, while also toxic, accumulates in flesh rather than fat, which is why both farmed and wild salmon tend to contain comparable levels of it.

Wild salmon may seem like the obvious choice here, but they are a highly limited, ever-shrinking resource. The oceans today are so overfished in general that some experts predict they will be effectively barren within forty years. The larger we grow as a species, the more our options for good, clean,

---

* Their sole North American producer was Monsanto. Just saying.

relatively guilt-free protein sources seem to dwindle and to increase in price.

Discussing the nutritional properties of two thousand edible insect species, many with specialized foods and ecosystems, is a bit like listing the hobbies of the human population—there is a certain amount of legitimate generalization, but also a very great deal of range. Like with any animal, diet plays a huge part in the nutritional profiles of insects. Still, there are some commonalities. Most insects tend to be high in zinc, an essential nutrient for immune system support, the lack of which has been identified as a core public health problem by the World Health Organization.

Aquatic insects tend to have higher levels of essential fatty acids, though all edible insects contain them to some extent. Many insects, such as crickets, grasshoppers, ants and certain caterpillars, are exceedingly high in calcium. Soldier fly larvae, used for processing compost, are off the charts in this nutrient.

As you may be aware, the nutrient B_{12} can only be found in animal sources. Crickets and cockroach nymphs are both impressively good sources for B_{12}, as you'll see in the chart on page 67. If vegans could accept the idea of eating insects, they could potentially manage their B_{12} intake just by popping a few crickets a couple times a week.

Part of the reason nutrient levels are so high for certain insects is because they are eaten whole, including their exoskeleton and internal organs. Certainly, if more of our livestock were somehow ground up whole and fed to us, we'd get far more nutrition out of them.

Calcium in particular may be high because of the fact that we ingest the insects' "bones," or exoskeleton. This protective structure is made out of chitin, a long-chain polymer of acetylglucosamine. It's the same stuff that shrimp, crab, and lobster shells are made of, as well as the cell walls of fungi (mushrooms). It is structurally similar to cellulose, which makes up the cell walls of plants, and functionally similar to keratin, which our hair and nails are made of. After cellulose, it is the second most abundant natural biopolymer on the planet, and is useful in things like biodegradable surgical thread, edible films for preserving fruits and vegetables, as a dietary fiber, and as a potential absorber of cholesterol.

Insect agriculture is a relatively new science. Different feeds and rearing environments affect the nutrient levels found in various insect species, so there are still conflicting and/or sparse data on their exact nutritional components. I have synthesized this information from several sources and adapted it into the chart on the facing page. These measures will give a rough idea of our current knowledge on the subject.

In one episode of *The Simpsons,* Lisa Simpson faints during a saxophone solo. The doctor chalks it up to an iron deficiency.

"Please say it's the vegetarianism," her mother prays.

"It's not the vegetarianism," snaps Lisa.

"It's a little bit the vegetarianism," says the doctor, prescribing iron supplements that clank like railroad spikes into his hand.

Lisa tries taking the monster supplements but complains of vitamin burps all day. Lunchlady Doris intervenes, giving Lisa a taste of what, she says, keeps her young: beetle mush. Lisa protests that she's a vegetarian.

"Get real," scoffs Doris. "There's bug parts in peanut butter!"

As the episode continues, Lisa joins Springfield's Insec-

Nutritional table

Source	Protein g	Fat g	Calcium	Iron	Zinc	Potassium	Niacin	Magnesium	B_{12} (mcg)
Cricket	20.5	6.8	40.7	1.9	6.7	347	3.8	33.7	5.4
Mealworm	23.7	5.4	23.1	2.2	4.6	340	5.6	60.6	0.5
Waxworm	14.1	24.9	24.3	5	2.5	221	3.7	31.6	0.1
Soldier Fly Larvae	17.5	14	934.2	6.6	13	453	7.1	40	5.5
Silkworm	9.3	1.4	17.7	1.6	3.1	316	2.6	49.8	0.1
Cockroach Nymph	19	10	38	1.4	3.2	224	4.4	50	23.7
Earthworm	10.5	1.6	44	5.4	1.7	182	N/A	13.6	N/A
House Fly	19.7	1.9	76	12.5	8.5	303	9	80.6	0.6
Chicken, skinless	21	3	12	0.9	1.5	229	8.2	25	0.4
Beef, 90% lean, ground	26.1	11.7	13	2.7	6.3	333	5.6	22	2.1
Fish, Atlantic Wild Salmon	19.8	6.3	12	0.8	0.6	490	7.8	29	3.2

Values compiled from nutritional studies by Mark Finke, Dennis Oonincx, Julieta Ramos-Elorduy, May Berenbaum, and the USDA.

Figures are mg/100g, unless otherwise noted

N/A: Not applicable, trace amounts

tivorian Society and tries such dishes as Spider Cordon Bleu and Windshield Casserole. She begins raising grasshoppers in the basement. One night at dinner, she even considers eating shrimp, reasoning that like the grasshoppers, "they're both arthropods."

It's no coincidence that in 2010 I hosted a bar-bug-cue in Los Angeles, which was attended by Dan Greaney, a writer for *The Simpsons*. While grilling shish kebugs, we discussed the various nutritional properties of the species we had on hand. As I recall, Dan ate a scorpion. As whimsical as the *Simpsons* episode seems, they were right on the money—many species of insects are an excellent source of iron. Houseflies have a whopping five times the amount of iron in beef, so consider that the next time you swallow one by accident.

Currently, when doctors diagnose an iron deficiency, they either prescribe iron supplements or tell you to eat more red meat, usually both. Red meat is known as the most concentrated source of iron available. But imagine if you could eat just a fraction of the amount and get the same level of iron. It's like those old Total commercials: You have to eat *this many* bowls of the other cereal just to get the nutrition that's in one bowl of Total. Although in this case, the bowl is full of bugs.

In addition to being great nutrition for humans, insects also have great potential as livestock feed. All the animal protein that pigs, chickens, and fish need could be well supplemented with insects. Chickens already consume insects as often as they can. It's kind of amazing it's taken us this far to really pursue the idea, considering the fact that insects are already in our food anyway.

If you peruse the FDA's accepted food defect levels website, you'll find that pretty much all processed food has a surprising amount of ground-up bugs in it. Processed food, in this case, is anything that comes in a package: bread, cereal, pasta, condiments, candy, and so on.

Lunchlady Doris was right: There *are* bug parts in peanut butter—up to 30 insect fragments per 100 grams, in fact.

For chocolate, it can be anywhere from 60 to 90 fragments per 100 grams. Ground oregano can have 1,250 or more insect fragments per 10 grams.

I like to think of it in terms of a night out at a pizza restaurant. If wheat flour can have 75 fragments per 50 grams, or about a half cup; tomato paste can have 30 fly eggs per 100 grams,* or a quarter cup; and hops can average 2,500 aphids per 10 grams, then a meal of pizza and beer could result in, what, 100 fragments per person? Five bits of bug per bite?

If insects are in all of our processed food, that means we've been ingesting them our whole lives, since we were babies. Gerber Grasshopper and Onions, anyone?

David George Gordon, author of *The Eat-a-Bug Cookbook*, relates a great story about why ketchup bottles wear those paper collars. Before modern homogenization equipment was used to process foods, the darker-colored bug parts would float to the top of the ketchup bottle, leaving an unappetizing black ring. To cover this up, they added a paper ring around the top of the ketchup bottle so people wouldn't be grossed out when they went to season their fries. Nowadays, the bugs are mixed in a lot better, so they don't float to the top the way they used to, but for many brands of sauce, the paper collars remain.

Think about it—which tomatoes get cooked and mashed into ketchup? The pretty, shiny, flawless grocery store ones? Or is it more likely the holey, bruised, unsightly ones that might have a bug or two inside? The FDA knows it's not dangerous to have all these cooked, processed, incidental insects in our food. In fact, it could even be good for us. In *Animal,*

---

* "Waiter, there's a fly in my tomato soup." "Where?" *"Everywhere."*

Vegetable, Miracle: A Year of Food Life, Barbara Kingsolver's daughter Camille writes of early vegan Hindus:

> Even the ancient Hindu populations of India were not complete vegetarians—though they did not know this. Traditional harvesting techniques always left a substantial amount of insect parts, mostly termite larvae and eggs, in their grain supply. When vegan Hindu populations began moving to England, where food sanitation regulations are stricter, they began to suffer from a high incidence of anemia.

Remember that freak-out people had over Starbucks using (a very common) cochineal beetle–derived dye for the red coloring of its strawberry Frappuccino? While people were angrily discussing it over their lattes and espressos, they failed to realize that up to 10 percent of *coffee beans themselves* can be insect infested, even though this information is readily available on the internet.

Cochineal coloring, also known as carmine dye or Natural Red 4, was the go-to red dye for foods, drinks, fabrics, and cosmetics until fancy chemicals like Red Dye #40 were invented. It is still used commonly today, but is steadily being priced out of the market by cheaper synthetics. This may be why products such as Campari, which were originally colored with carmine dye, switched to an artificial dye a few years ago.

We intentionally use many other types of insect products in the foods we eat every day. Honey, for one, which, if you didn't know already, is actually bee vomit. Silk, of course, comes from the cocoons of silkworms, which is why PETA's against its use; in order to get silk, millions of baby silk moths have to die. The cocoons are boiled, and the dead pupae are removed and, in some cases, eaten as a snack on the factory floor. Shellac, or confectioners' glaze, is a resin secreted by the lac bug in the forests of Southeast Asia and is used as a coating for pills and candies like jellybeans. Yes, even Skittles used shellac from lac bugs on its candy until 2009. It's also used in combination with wax to make our apples look extra appealing.

Insects are an inextricable part of our lives and food chain. With so much positive evidence in their favor, it seems silly to continue to denigrate them as a food option, and certainly not with the open hostility we're accustomed to.

If aliens were to visit our planet without any preconceived notions about its life forms, they would probably find it quite quaint and amusing that Earth's most influential society runs screaming from the tiniest animals. How would we explain ourselves logically?

"Well, you see, *some* of them bite or sting, and you can never tell which . . ." This sort of reasoning would make us seem oddly unobservant at best, lazy and superstitious at worst.

I'm prospectively embarrassed for us just thinking about it.

4

You Are What You Eat Eats

D ADDY, HOW OLD was I when I ate my first bug?"
asks Max, Zack Lemann's twelve-year-old son.
Zack is the head chef at the Audubon Butterfly
Garden and Insectarium's Bug Appétit Café in New Orleans.
He helped start the Insectarium in 2008. It's the biggest bug
zoo in the United States and serves bugs to the public daily.

Zack whistles. "That's a good question," he says. "I think
you were about three."

I ask Max what his favorite bug to eat is.

"Dragonflies," says Max. "He"—he points to his dad—
"fries them in Zatarain's."

Zatarain's is a locally produced and famous Creole seasoning. Zack is well-known for his Cajun-styled bug recipes, like
Odonata Hors D'oeuvres—swamp-caught dragonflies coated
in cornmeal and Zatarain's and then sautéed in butter. Or his
Red Beans and Yikes, made with wax moth larvae instead of
rice. He once cooked bugs on *The Tonight Show with Jay Leno*.

I'm having dinner with Max and Zack at their stately

home on a muggy, mosquito-filled October evening. Tonight we're eating the duck they hunted together last fall. Tomorrow, Zack has promised to take me hunting for specimens for the Insectarium in the bottomland swamplands just brimming with things that crawl and slither and ooze. I can't wait.

The next morning we head out to the woods around the Audubon Species Survival Center, a place both visually and philosophically similar to Jurassic Park. Embryos of different animals are cryogenically frozen and stored here for research and conservation purposes. The wide, wooded grounds are home to a few live specimens and a fancy researcher's lodge, and are a fecund, favorite area of Zack's for bug collecting. The grounds are moist, verdant, and full of rotting wood. The latter is a good place to look for patent-leather beetles, our prime target.

Thwack!

That's the sound I hear as Zack splits open a rotten log in search of the beetles, which will be a great addition to the Insectarium's "bug petting zoo," where visitors can handle insects ranging from cockroaches to millipedes.

"From an educational standpoint, a bug in the hand is worth five in a jar, and five hundred pictures," Zack tells me. Rugged and muscular, dripping with sweat in the Louisiana heat, he looks like Indiana Jones. Then he opens his mouth, and he's Bill Nye the Science Guy. He does a great parody of Sir Mix-A-Lot's "Baby Got Back" song:

> *I like big bugs and I cannot lie*
> *You entomologists can't deny*
> *When a beetle flies in and does a little spin and lands*
> *   right on your* [collecting] *sheet you say*

*Please, let it be Dynastes, 'cause you know that bug
is cool.*

(It's on YouTube, and I highly recommend that you stop reading right now and go watch it. Then keep reading.)

The Insectarium, which Zack helped start, prides itself on
engaging visitors' five senses and provides an immersion learning experience. Visitors get to see displays of colorful insects,
hear their calls, handle them at interactivity stations, and even
smell and taste them in the Bug Appétit Café.

This immersion is far more likely to correct long-held
misconceptions about bugs than just reading about them in
a book. For example, when you hold a patent-leather beetle,
you can really tell just how harmless and even friendly they
are: They're slow moving and gentle, and will trudge across
your hand as you turn it over, like a treadmill, again and again.
You're likely to get bored well before the beetle does. They're
also good candidates for the interactivity stations (a.k.a. bug-
petting spots) because they live long and are hardy. They can
last for a couple of years in captivity, don't seem to be affected
by constant touching, and require only rotting wood for
food. And they're pretty, in their way—black and shiny and
smooth, clean as bullets. Patent-leather beetles rarely use their
wings; in fact, most only use them once in their lives, like a
wedding dress: on their nuptial flight to mate before return-
ing to the land of log.

Over fallen trunks and under hanging branches, to bee-
tle-infested logs we go. I can barely keep up with Zack as he
scuttles expertly through the thick evergreen forest. The air itself is thick, too, with mosquitoes and humidity. The threat of
autumn rain looms. I slap at a mosquito that has landed on

my unprotected right temple. "Bastards," I mutter. Mosquitoes are the one bug I can definitely do without. They're nothing but bloodsucking, disease-ridden pests.

"Actually, these are all bitches," Zack tells me, not breaking his log-snapping rhythm. "Male mosquitoes don't bite.
Females only suck blood to gather protein to make eggs. In
fact, mosquitoes, if they feed at all, drink nectar."

I didn't know that. Of course, being flower-feeders, mosquitoes also contribute to pollination. There goes another
insect we thought was good for nothing but irritation. And
itching. I guiltily brush the dead mosquito off my pants leg,
mentally whispering an apology.

"Ah, here's a good log," says Zack as he plunges his hands
fearlessly into a pile of decomposing wood. There's no time
to think about what's climbing up my legs or landing on my
neck as I snap photographs, take notes, and supply Zack with
collecting vials for the beetles and other bugs he pulls out of
the logs, the air, and the branches around us. One of them is
a large bumblebee, which now buzzes, muted, in its own glass
vial in a net pocket of Zack's waist pack. I keep an eye on it.

"Yes!" he crows triumphantly, pulling two shiny, inch-and-
a-half-long black grooved beetles out of tunnels in the spongy
pecan wood. He holds one up first to his ear, then to mine.
"Hear that?" he asks. The beetle is squeaking, almost like a
mouse, if a mouse had rusty hinges for vocal cords. "That's
how they talk to each other. They rub their wings together,
and the vibrations travel through the wood, communicating
with the other beetles in the colony. These are a surprisingly
social species."

A patent-leather beetle mother (not a word often associated with bugs) will chew up wood to feed to her children until they pupate, hatching into beetles. Then she'll spend up to

a year—a good portion of her life—feeding and tending to them. For humans, that would be like nursing your kid until he or she was thirty.

Communicating via vibrations and chewing up food to feed to their young makes the patent-leather beetle sound like a cross between a whale and a bird—both animals we have a lot of empathy for. But somehow we're surprised to find social and motherly instincts in such a tiny, hard-shelled, and, well, patent-leathery insect.

Zack digs into more wood, which is so soft it splits like bread in his hands. When he squeezes it, gray water runs down his wrist. I crouch down to get a close shot of the pair of beetles before they wander off and hear Zack snort loudly. I look up to see him holding a fat white scarab larva under his right nostril, like the biggest, lumpiest booger you ever saw. He mugs for the camera, then puts the grub in my palm.

The larva squirms weakly on its back, opening and closing its jaws, for all the world like a sleepy, protesting puppy roused from a nap. Its creamy-colored insides are plainly visible beneath translucent skin. I ask Zack if it's edible.

"Sure," he says. "But it tastes like wood."

Just then, thunder rumbles, followed by a silver flash and the sound of rain pattering. We quickly gather up our equipment and scamper out of the woods to the safety of Zack's truck. We throw everything haphazardly into the Range Rover and slam the doors against the downpour.

As I'm putting the collecting jars into a bag, the top of the one holding the giant bumblebee comes off.

"Shit! Shit!" I say, scrambling to mash the cap back on before the inch-long carpenter bee gets loose in the car.

"If it's any consolation," says Zack calmly, "I've never known those to be vindictive. She's more likely to be disoriented, like, 'I was in a jar! Now I'm in a car!' and not, 'Oh, look, a large warm-blooded animal. I think I'll sting the snot out of it just because.'" Laughing helps dispel the shaking in my hands. My own bug prejudices were laid bare at the thought of being stung by a bumblebee. Maybe I could use a day at the Insectarium learning a little more of the bug psychology that Zack seems to grasp so intuitively. These are not, as my fear seems to assume, horrific killing machines. They have varied personalities and priorities, surprisingly few of which involve harming humans in any way. And yet we treat them like alien invaders.

The Insectarium, at the corner of Decatur and Canal Streets, just inside the border of New Orleans' French Quarter, looks, from the outside, far more federal than fun. On the ground floor of the old US Customs House, its penitentiary-gray granite walls are broken by barred windows and haughty Egyptian columns. But from the sidewalk, you can see bottle-blue, red, and yellow butterflies flapping behind those barred windows, flits of color peeking out from within the stony building.

"We've started calling it the Audubon Butterfly Garden and Insectarium," says entomologist Jayme Necaise, the director of animals and visitor programs. "It's more popular that way."

Everyone loves butterflies, right? Indeed, as Jayme leads me on a tour of the center, two different groups ask him how to get to the butterflies. "We're not even halfway through," Jayme groans after giving them directions to follow the U of the museum trail to its end. "They're going to miss all the best stuff."

Once through the building's dour entrance, the atmosphere erupts into color. Giant plastic insects adorn the walls, and striking displays of insect life cycles and notable species draw the eye every which way. Glassed-in exhibit tanks hold large discoid cave roaches, glittering rainbow jewel beetles, long wavering stick insects, and extremely rare pink katydids, which the Insectarium alone has been able to raise in captivity. At one large enclosure, you can watch as red leaf-cutter ants go industriously about their business, carrying green bits of mulberry leaf up a branch into their nest like slow-motion, upwardly mobile confetti.

Jayme sticks his finger into a small, random hole drilled in the glass display of American cockroaches, which is made to look like a kitchen pantry full of cans of food, jars, and sacks of flour and sugar. And, of course, it's crawling with cockroaches.

"People freak out about this little hole all the time. They pull me aside and say, 'Look, the roaches can get out!'" He shows me where the roach enclosure closes off just before the hole.

"Actually," Jayme continues, "sometimes we will find roaches loose around this exhibit. But they aren't ours— they're 'wild' roaches who come to hang out with ours. Because ours are the 'cool' roaches."

Roaches, like the patent-leather beetles, are surprisingly social and like to be around their brethren. I mention to Jayme that it's interesting how averse people are to insects, even avoiding them at all costs, while in many cases, it's the closest to wildlife they'll ever get.

"That's true," says Jayme. "You may never get to see a Bengal tiger, but you've got roaches living right under your fridge."

Finally, we arrive at the display I've come two thousand

miles to see: Bug Appétit, one of the only places in the country that serves bugs as food to the public seven days a week.

Mack and Moni, two of the Insectarium's staff bug cooks, tell me that until recently there was a kind of bug buffet available all day from the museum's open at 10 A.M. till close at 5 P.M. About six weeks ago, however, they switched to the "show" system. Now, instead, you can see a real live bug cooking show, complete with info slides and samples, three times a day.

"It's much easier to get an actual message about edible insects across that way," says Zack "Before, people would come by and either try things or freak out without really knowing the background on it. This way we can tell them what and why and really engage them."

Before the show system, menu options also included Bugyays (beignets made with mealworms), Six-Legged Salsa, Crispy Cajun Crickets, Cinnamon Bug Crunch, Chocolate Chirp Cookies, and the Odonata Hors D'oeuvres (fried dragonflies with mustard sauce). Many of these are still served on a regular basis, but not all.

"I used to come in on Sundays and make banana-cricket fritters," says Jayme.

"Aw, man!" I wail. "You mean I could've come in and had cricket fritters for breakfast?!"

"Yup," says Jayme. The other chefs grin.

The next day, Monday morning, I accompany Zack to get the week's worth of food for the Insectarium's inhabitants.

Zack cuts passionflower vines from his neighbor's fence, pulls off next to the train tracks for some red-tip photinia, and then heads into a grocery store for mushrooms. Then we're off to the Audubon Zoo's commissary for the rest of the produce. In the giant walk-in refrigerator, Zack chats with some women cutting up vegetables for the primates while he piles apples, grapes, oranges, several bunches of bananas, a cantaloupe, and seven heads of lettuce into a cardboard box.

The truck looks like we are about to start a juice cleanse and it strikes me: This is what bugs eat. This is what they are.

They say you are what you eat. But aren't you also what what you eat eats? Does the fact that the middleman sports an exoskeleton really matter?

It's a simple fact that many of the bugs we hate the most are the ones that eat what we eat, the ones that perhaps even compete with us for food. Perhaps that's why a general rule of science fiction is that there are certain things the hero can kill with abandon, without moral judgment: robots, the undead, monsters, Nazis, and insects. In our haste to eradicate the threat we perceive them posing to our farms and gardens, we tend to attack them with the environmental version of chemotherapy: pesticides. In our effort to aggressively target one aspect of the ecosystem, we often wind up negatively affecting other parts of it.

Chemotherapy fights cancer by causing cell apoptosis, a mechanism that is pretty much what it sounds like. The cells basically pop, shattering into pieces. People with cancer are actually taught to envision this process as part of holistic healing. No one cares what happens to cancer cells—they're 100 percent bad, and as single cells, they don't have feelings. Insects, though, are living beings.

I think we can all agree that pulling the wings off a fly is a shitty thing to do. Yet we have no problem spraying Raid on a roach or dousing a farm with pesticide. We just never think about what happens to the insect after we've done so.

In *The Vegetarian Myth: Food, Justice, and Sustainability,* author Lierre Keith tells a story of trying to grow her own food in her garden. In her quest for vegan, cruelty-free food, she notices that her plants, free of pesticides and vulnerable to the world, are soon besieged by the Gardener's Grievance: slugs. Keith tries to look the other way, but quickly becomes aware of how much damage the slugs are doing. If left to their own slimy devices, they will devastate her crops and reduce her yield to almost nothing. Since Keith isn't running a soup kitchen for slugs, she begins brainstorming ways to gently bounce her uninvited guests.

At first, she plucks them off by hand, puts them into buckets, and actually drives them out to the countryside to set them free, like you would with an opossum that had wandered into your yard. Upon arriving, she realizes that the forest, being its own ecosystem, already has its fill of slugs. Ecosystems tend to fill every niche, so by releasing her garden slugs, which had been drawn in by her artificially created bounty, she is simply throwing another ecosystem out of balance. More likely, though, the slugs would starve to death.

Most people would probably be okay with this second option. After all, they're just crawling bags of slime, aren't they? But Keith isn't satisfied with this answer.

In searching for a more humane solution to her bug problem, she reads about a miracle product called diatomaceous earth, which is organic and doesn't hurt the other organisms growing in the garden. She thinks she has solved her problem, until she does further research and discovers that diatomaceous earth, fragments of siliceous rock, works by essentially slicing up the slugs' bellies as they slide along the ground. They are eventually desiccated to death.

Far from the first person to deal with the issue of how to deter garden pests, Keith wonders why the impossibility of doing so humanely isn't talked about, even among those urban-gardening, kombucha-drinking, vegan yogi types who mainly seem to exercise so they can reproduce those "I'd rather wear nothing than wear fur" ads from the '80s.

She concludes it is because slugs can't scream. But like us (well, like some of us), slugs make love for hours during mating, caressing each other all over in a sensual, viscous contact love dance. They build homes and return to them every night. They cannot, however, express discomfort vocally, unlike cows, pigs, chickens, and others high on PETA's list.* They also aren't very cuddly. All that stuff about "not killing anything with a face or a mother" doesn't seem to extend to invertebrates, who definitely have mothers and definitely have a face of sorts—just one drastically different from our own. So even though the "face" phrase is supposed to be about loving animals, isn't this just another form of anthrocentrism— the idea that only those with a lot in common with humans deserve humane treatment?

Keith finally settles on beer: Slugs love it and will crawl into it and drown. She figures at least they will die happy.

---

* To be fair, PETA does care about bugs. They advise against wearing silk because it requires the deaths of millions of silkworms; they don't believe in stealing honey from bees; they recommend natural pest deterrents whenever possible. They even ask you not to harm insects unless absolutely necessary. When recommending the use of orange oil to repel ants, they ask you not to put it directly on the ants: "[W]hen applied directly to ants, the active ingredient d-Limonene (orange peel extract) destroys the waxy coating of the insects' respiratory systems, causing the ants to suffocate, so please do not spray ants with the repellent. Simply spray the repellent around your home—the citrus fragrance of d-Limonene will repel the ants without killing them." Isn't that sweet?

But no matter what, in order to save her vegetables for herself, Keith is forced to acknowledge that she has blood on her hands.

Most of us tend to blindly invoke the Raids and Regents of the world without thinking about how, exactly, they do their dirty deeds. Keith is a rare exception, and her example bears exploring. Have you ever thought about what pesticides actually *do*?

It's all right there in the name: *-cide,* a suffix that comes from the Latin word *caedere,* meaning "to kill." When you decide to do something, you "kill" off your other options. It has a negative connotation when combined with *geno-, homi-,* and *infanti-,* but is heard as useful when paired with *insecti-, pesti-,* or *fungi-.*

When we think negatively of pesticides, we tend to think of the ills they cause to things we deem valuable, such as the environment (rivers, streams), animals like songbirds (see: *Silent Spring*), our water supply, and, ultimately, us. Pesticides have been linked to various cancers, endocrine problems, and poorer health in general. They are impossible to contain—traces of DDT have been found in animals living in the deep sea and are present in the breast milk of every nursing female animal on Earth, including humans.

Beyond these more macro effects, we tend to think of pesticides as necessary evils, if we think about them at all. But what about their targets? When you think of a crop duster flying over a field, raining poison on the insects chomping merrily away below, what do you imagine happens to the bugs themselves?

Most people have never thought about this side of the equation. But when pressed—at least among those *I've* pressed on the subject—they tend to think it goes something like this: The pesticides fall upon the crops, and then the insects go into teeny little coughing fits. They choke and splutter on the fumes, losing their tiny grips on the plants they were eating. They fall to the ground, gasping and reaching toward the light like fatally injured soldiers, close their eyes, and fall into the Deep Sleep. The soil wraps around their tiny bodies, pulling them gently under, where the plant roots can recycle them back into the food chain.

Am I close?

But that's not the reality. Pesticides work in all sorts of morbid ways. Insects die of paralysis, starvation, suffocation, stomach poisoning, and desiccation—things you wouldn't wish on your worst enemy. Whether it "hurts" them is up for debate. On the one hand, insects are incredibly sensitive— ever try to catch a fly? They have nerves, message channels that transmit sensory information, which start at their extremities and end in their brains, just like ours do. Flies actually process time several times faster than we do, perceiving our seemingly fast-approaching hand as coming at them in slow motion. Their sensory trains definitely arrive at the station (and are bullet trains compared to our poky local ones, at that), but then what?

On the other hand, insects have a much simpler version, a dot-and-line drawing, of our own complex anatomy. They lack the complex brain to process sensory input like we do. For us, the problem with pain as we know it is that it means something—it means we are sick or injured, that something is wrong. This is perceived as negative by us, because we're so darned complex—we've invested a lot in our mammalian lives. However, if you are hurt, but can't or don't process it, and/or have a very short lifespan, does it "matter"?

Hey, I'm guilty of being intentionally fuzzy on this myself.

Despite my official stance on the subject, when I find families of aphids hunkering down on my kale plants, I spray the heck out of them. I use plain water, because I know all that stuff about, you know, violent, horrible death—and because I want to keep my plants organic, I spritz them off into oblivion, and my thought process stops there. In fact, I may even feel the tiniest sense of righteous satisfaction. Maybe. But you didn't hear it from me. But when I do this, even with just water, I'm blasting those aphids off the only homes they've ever known, like an alien with a giant ray gun. They hit the dry, nonnutritive dirt, and probably, most of them starve to death. They were born and raised on that kale, but are granted no rights to it.

My point is that insects usually fall below our collective empathic range. Most of us have absolutely never considered what happens after we deploy our bug deterrents. It's as if they lived in another dimension.

I'm not saying we shouldn't use pesticides or pest deterrents of any kind. I'm not saying we should become like the Jains of India, carefully sweeping bugs out of the way of our every measured step. I do think we should realize what we are doing when we kill bugs—that, indeed, we *are* killing them and causing them to suffer whenever we grow crops. And it doesn't stop there. Many, many animals and other organisms have to die in order for our crops to grow, from the cute-and-fuzzy to the squirmy-and-slimy variety. Every species on Earth does the best it can to survive, and growing crops is part of our survival. An awareness of what it costs helps us stay in balance with our environment enough to create long-term, sustainable practices.

Practices, perhaps, like eating the extra protein crop pests contain instead of destroying it.

5

The Breakup

JOHN BENDER: [pointing to Claire's lunch]
What's that?
CLAIRE STANDISH: Sushi.
JOHN: Sushi?
CLAIRE: Rice, raw fish, and seaweed.
JOHN: You won't accept a guy's tongue in your
mouth, and you're going to eat that?

— THE BREAKFAST CLUB

I T's 10:30 A.M. on a Tuesday, and I'm up to my elbows in
a bucket of rotting corn, searching for caterpillars. Corn
earworms, larvae of the *Helicoverpa zea* moth, to be exact.
After being turned down by nearly every organic farm in
the area, Veggielution Community Farm in San Jose, California, has graciously agreed to let me harvest this crawling protein that might have otherwise gone to the chickens. Next to
me, two volunteers sit on the blue picnic table bench, shuck-
ing and chopping corn ears to sell at the weekly farm stand,

chucking the corn tops into my bucket. Veggielution is a non-profit, six-acre pocket of urban community agriculture tucked below a highway overpass in Northern California, just east of bustling central San Jose, at the southern end of Silicon Valley.

Highways 101 and 280 crisscross in the near distance above the reaching tips of the corn, a dramatically industrial back-drop to the rows of red chard, fava beans, tomatoes, beets, kale, carrots, and fennel. The constant white noise *whoosh* of traffic blends with the clucking conversations of free-roaming chickens, punctuated occasionally by the crowing of roosters and the snarl of semis. Peahens wander en masse from patch to patch of vegetables, eating all the knee-level-and-below bugs, while solitary peacocks patrol the grounds, proud as swaggering western sheriffs.

"The peacocks are the real pests," one of the volunteers tells me. "In the spring, they aggressively show off their tail feathers to the tours of schoolkids and freak them out."

In your face, peacocks, I think, pulling out more of the worm-eaten corn tops the volunteers toss into my blue bucket. I extract the big green, brown, and sometimes pink-ish-orange-striped caterpillars that bite. The bigger and more solitary the caterpillar, the more of its brethren it probably has consumed along with the corn. Corn earworms, once they reach a certain stage, become cannibalistic, literally eat-ing up the competition. *Worms within worms,* I think, pulling a particularly fat green one out of its cozy corn-top home and dropping it into my Tupperware bowl.

When I went to study pre-Columbian traditional food and medicine in Mexico as a college student, in addition to the bugs I ate, I also got to see an ancient Aztec god in daily practice—corn.

Corn's significance in ancient and modern Mexican, American, and global history cannot be overstated. (I promise, just a quick history lesson on this most influential of crops, and then we'll get back to the bugs.) First domesticated in Mexico's Central Balsas River Valley around eighty-seven hundred years ago, what we know today as corn began as a slender, tasseled grass called teosinte.

Through human observation, intervention, and finally domestication, teosinte began to produce an edible crop more reliably, with bigger and more palatable kernels. As much as wheat was the staff of life in the Middle East, corn was the staff of life here in the Americas—and continues to be to this day. People in Mexico still occasionally call themselves "corn walking."

As corn was domesticated into the thick, heavy cobs we know it as today, the corn earworm came right along with it. The moment corn became a viable food source, along came the pests, much like with any other boon. The Aztecs, however, took a different perspective on the intruder or, should we say, "bonus crop." In their opinion, an ear of corn with a worm in it was considered better than one without.* This wisdom is still commonly felt today, even in the United States, though in a different bent: An ear of sweet corn neglected by the worms is thought to be of lesser taste and quality. The worms know their corn.

The idea of putting an undesirable or unintentional agricultural by-product to good use has been employed by other cultures for centuries. *Huitlacoche,* or corn smut, is a bluish-black tumorlike fungus that infects corn crops during periods

---

* It's true: The proteins in the worm would have complemented the amino acids in the corn, resulting in a more nutritionally complete meal.

of drought; it's often called "raven's excrement" because of its appearance. US farmers generally regard it as a blight, but it is sold as a delicacy in Mexico, where infected ears sell for a significantly higher price at market. A popular filling for quesadillas, it has a subtle, earthy, mushroomy taste and is high in lysine, which corn lacks almost totally. Combining corn with lysine-rich *huitlacoche* gives it a more complete amino acid profile. In the '90s, the USDA cooperated on a marketing program, introducing *huitlacoche* as the "Mexican truffle" to help put the fungus to good use. Today, a few US farmers make a modest living selling it.

Noting the widespread use of pesticides in industrial agriculture, *Food Insects Newsletter* founder Gene DeFoliart said, "People are poisoning the planet by ridding it of insects, rather than eating insects and keeping artificial chemicals off plants that we eat."

Five hundred years ago, pests like corn earworms were included in the diet, not deducted from it. The protein into which the caterpillars transformed the corn was not wasted but integrated. Granted, at Veggielution, the caterpillars would have gone to the chickens to be transformed into eggs, but at the majority of farms, they are eradicated. Because they are protected within the safe harbor of the husk, it's logistically difficult to kill corn worms with insecticide without harming the corn. Thus handpicking, like I'm doing today, has become a preferred method of removal—particularly for organic, poly-cropping farms like Veggielution.

Each corn top is like opening a present—unwrapping the layers of papery green husk to see if anyone's inside. The soft, mealy, worm-eaten bits of corn flatten into the folds of husk resemble, more than anything else, the masa or corn flour from which tamales and tortillas and, heck, much of Mexican food is made. I wonder about the origin of tamales in particular as I scoop out the hunks of this natural masa, as well as the caterpillars that made it and would make an obvious natural filling.

The Aztec Nahuatl word for "caterpillar tamale" is *ocuiltamalli*. What kind of caterpillars they used in these tamales is up to the interpretation of more dedicated historians than I, but it's likely the list included the omnipresent earworm as well as the *gusano,* a.k.a. the agave caterpillar or "tequila worm." The worm in the tequila bottle, by the way, is not a worm, nor was it traditionally found in tequila bottles. It was originally a *gusano,* the caterpillar that feeds on the agave plant. Agave is used to make mezcal, tequila's smokier, rougher, less-processed precursor.*

Early mezcal brewers included the caterpillar in the bottle for two reasons: one, to prove that the mezcal was indeed made from agave and not some other fermented ingredient, and two, that the mezcal was of sufficiently high alcohol content to preserve the body of the insect. In other words, the caterpillar served as a form of grade labeling for purity and strength. It has no more hallucinogenic properties than a whiskey-soaked sausage.

I wanted to flip Western history on its head by taking some of these corn caterpillars and bringing them to the table, much as the ancient Aztecs might have, and as agriculturalists around the world have done with their own crop pests. Farm-

---

* The sequence actually goes like this: First, the heart of the agave plant is cut out. Left to its own devices, this exposed center fills with liquid, the "blood" or "milk" of the plant. This liquid ferments naturally, producing a slightly alcoholic but nutritious sour-sweet beverage the early Mexicans called pulque, which was drunk by all generations. Further fermentation and processing creates mezcal, pulque's harder big sister. Later, smoothing industrialization gave us tequila, pulque and mezcal's more stable, commercially popular relative.

ers in Thailand have been known to fetch more at the market for the grasshoppers that feed on their rice crops than the rice itself, while African farmers get more for mopane caterpillars, the larvae of the emperor moth, than beef. Corn smut may not be popular with the US palate, but corn earworms are universal and exist even on healthy ears of corn.

My little Tupperware containers are swiftly filling up with caterpillars of many colors and sizes. I make sure to drop plenty of corn kernels and husks in there, to prevent them from attacking and eating each other, as they are wont to do whenever they bump chitin. Unbeknownst to me, one has crawled up the inside of my shirtsleeve and bites down on the tender skin near my armpit. The sudden sharp sting makes me yelp and rip off my overshirt to remove the intruder. It didn't hurt much—not more than getting pricked by a thorn or berry bramble, but I can imagine what it must feel like to a much smaller, soft-bodied caterpillar. I toss some more kernels and husks into my containers.

After about thirty minutes of picking through one batch of corn tops, I have a couple dozen fat caterpillars. Not a huge harvest, but a reasonable amount to make a special dish of them. I'm thinking tamales.

My farm-pest-to-table scheme gets legs when I meet with Treena Joi for lemonade at her artful Mountain View apartment. Treena, a middle school science teacher, has been serving bugs to the public for more than fifteen years. For the past three, she has collaborated on a gourmet bug banquet for Stanford alumni at the exclusive University Club of San Francisco. Perfect.

Treena says she started out eating bugs for "economic reasons"—as a struggling young entomology student at Humboldt State University in Northern California, they presented a cheap source of protein.

"I saw a travel show where this guy goes to the outback in Australia and eats witchetty grubs. It looked like lobster to me. I couldn't afford lobster, and I couldn't find witchetty grubs in Northern California, but I could catch grasshoppers."

As we sit down to echinacea lemonade in her bug-bedazzled abode, Treena tells me about some of the first dinners she served to her fellow entomology students.

"We'd have these potlucks, and, you know, it was Humboldt." Humboldt is known for being a very "green" region, in all senses of the word. Giant redwoods, eco-friendliness, hippies, and marijuana abound. "So there'd be the regular lasagna, the vegan lasagna—of course, everything was labeled— the regular brownies, the pot brownies, the regular stuffed mushrooms, and the ant-stuffed mushrooms." She laughs. "Sometimes people would ask me things like, 'What are the ants made of?' And I'd say, 'Ants.'"

Today, Treena teaches middle school science in Portola Valley, California, the more rural western edge of the Palo Alto area and one of the wealthiest areas in the country, where the houses are large, the lots are wooded, and much of the money comes from tech start-ups in Silicon Valley. She has been including edible insects in her curriculum since she started there in 2002.

"I used to do a bug buffet every year for Earth Day in April," she says. "But now the kids start badgering me about it from the first day of school. 'Ms. Joi, when are we going to eat bugs? Ms. Joi, do you have any bugs for us to eat right now?' They can't wait. So I try to hold out as long as I can, which is about October at this point."

Considering school starts in September, that's not much of a holdout.

I ask Treena how the bugs are usually received.

"I tell the kids, 'No screaming, no whining, and no crying.' If they don't like a bug, they can quietly go spit it out, but they can't start shrieking about it, because that spreads like a virus. Usually, once a couple of the popular kids have given it the okay, the rest follow."

Just what I've been thinking all along. If popular Western society could accept the idea of eating insects they would likely help the rest of the world follow.

A few nights later, I'm up at midnight making corn caterpillar tamales. The Stanford alumni dinner Treena invited me to is tomorrow evening, and I'm hoping that my first attempt at making tamales will be successful. I have *Radiolab* on and am listening to an episode on the potentially positive health effects of parasites while I sauté the caterpillars.

I am impressed with how easy it was to collect the ingredients for tonight's culinary venture (excluding, of course, the caterpillars—that took an impressive amount of tenacity and persuasion). I had gone to my favorite Latin American market and was thrilled to see that it practically had a kit for making tamales. Bags of dried corn husks sat next to balls of string, and sacks of corn flour were labeled FOR TAMALES. All the ingredients together wound up costing about $10, with plenty of extra left over for another round.

I try to go as traditional as possible on the tamale filling, but after searching a bunch of recipes online and in books, I give up. There's nothing else I can find that quite matches the consistency of the caterpillars, so I just make something up. This makes it sound as if I'm a naturally good cook, like

I have some genius in the kitchen or something. Let me tell you, I'm not that person, and you don't have to be, either. I am creative, however, and I've cooked enough bugs at this point that I have some idea of what works. As with many foods, you generally can't go wrong with onions and garlic.

I start out by sautéeing the onions in butter, letting them soften and brown a little while I chop the garlic and slice kernels off raw corncobs. I finely dice a habanero, feeling the burn on my fingertips as I toss it in the pan. Once everything else has had a chance to cook a bit, I carefully add in the frozen caterpillars, which have held up well since the harvesting several weeks ago. Just like the wax worms do, the multicolored earworms straighten out and plump up in the heat. They look delicious, actually, and I pick one out and pop it in my mouth. It tastes green and corn-y and slightly bitter, as if I'd taken a bite straight from a raw corncob. I nod to myself. This was pretty much what I'd expected. It was really quite good, like a shrimp crossed with raw corn.

Once everything is sautéed, I begin spreading the masa dough onto the corn husks. I spoon a little of the sauté mixture onto the dough and roll the whole thing together, not unlike the sushi rolls I used to practice making when I worked at a Japanese restaurant. After a couple of tries, I get the process down. When you roll them right, corn husks fold up so naturally into tamale envelopes that it really does seem as if Centeotl, the Aztec god of corn, designed them that way. Cornigami. I tie them off with the string, like tiny Christmas presents, and plunk them into the steamer. It's quite fun. I'm having such a good time that I don't notice that it's nearly two A.M. before I'm done.

The next night, I head up to San Francisco, proudly toting my buggy booty in an insulated bag to keep it warm. A

streetcar clangs as I duck into the University Club, at the top
of windy, rainy Nob Hill. Founded in 1890, the club was originally created as a space for college-educated gentlemen to live
and conduct their social affairs—as the Club's website remi-
nisces, San Francisco's many restaurants "were not the chosen
venue of a gentleman unless a private room was available: in
the absence of other distractions, the highlight of most organized nights was an after-dinner speech; this was the great age
of after-dinner speaking."

Today it's used for university events like the one tonight,
which features before-dinner PowerPoint presentations on
entomophagy instead of after-dinner speeches. I wrestle my
myriad bags past the curious eyes of the doorman and into the
warm, cozily lit lobby, where I pick up a name tag identifying
me as a Stanford alum. *Easiest degree I ever earned,* I think,
hauling my load up the emerald carpeted stairs. In truth,
I'm the only non-Stanford grad allowed at this thing. Treena
is already there, setting up dishes of crackers with hummus
topped with mealworms and toasted crickets.

The event takes place in the library, and it's exactly as you
might imagine: dark wood paneling, a big fireplace, and floor-
to-ceiling built-in bookcases full of old leather-bound books.
Chandeliers cast a warm glow upon the clusters of chatting
attendees; there's a palpable nervous giddiness in the room
as people sip artisan beer and martinis. The air of the nine-
teenth-century gentleman certainly remains, and everyone
stands up a little straighter, as if they're being sternly observed
by the ruler-straight, elegant surroundings. The twinkling, ex-
pansive view of San Francisco from the fourth-floor windows
completes the feeling of old-money privilege.

The spread is equally impressive. There are gorgeous apple galettes and pear tarts sprinkled with fly pupae that look

like forbidden black rice; tiny polenta towers topped with sun-dried tomatoes and giant super mealworms; and crystal goblets filled with various roasted arthropods: spicy *chapulines* from Mexico, lemon-roasted crickets, toasted wax moth larvae, and *nsenene*, fried katydids from Africa. I note Dave Gracer's work—he's the only one I know who imports some of these species. I arrange my tamales on a plate next to a bowl of chipotle blackberry salsa, and slice up a bright fuchsia cactus pear for color.

As Treena preps for her presentation, I walk around the room, introducing myself and asking people what brought them here tonight. I mean, they've paid $45 a head to be here, to eat bugs.

"You only live once," says an alum named Karen, here with her best friend, Sarah. They laugh that there's comfort in doing it together.

"It's something different. And it's been coordinated as a social outing by Stanford. So it's a fun, safe way to try something new."

"We're all going to be doing it in ten years anyway," says Tony Shen, an economics grad. "I thought it would be interesting to challenge myself."

"I love the contrast," adds Mike Francis, grinning. "Here we are in this rich mahogany room with leather-bound books, eating bugs."

Most people at tonight's dinner haven't eaten insects before. But for entrepreneur Wilson Tandiono, it's a throwback to his childhood in Indonesia: "We used to put buckets of water under lights. Mayflies would come to the light and then fall into the water. We'd scoop them out and fry them. They were good."

Treena calls the room to order and dims the lights for the

projector. She gives an entertaining and in-depth talk about entomophagy worldwide, to the many oohs, aahs, and nervous giggles of the audience. They are particularly moved by the photographs of witchetty grubs that she shows—the insect that inspired her to begin studying entomophagy in the first place. Everyone leans closer to get a look at the big white grubs on the projector screen.

"I just thought they looked so nummers," Treena says with a laugh.

When it's my turn, I tell the room that I'm conducting a social experiment—instead of just farm to table, I've brought them farm pest to table. The whole shebang. They groan. I hold up my hands and explain that by serving them tamales made with corn caterpillars, which have essentially eaten nothing else in their lives except corn, and have in fact lived their entire lives on and around corn, they'll be eating corn wrapped in corn wrapped in corn. They like that idea.

Pesticide usage has not necessarily increased our agricultural output—in fact, it's just the opposite. In the seventy-plus years since we began aggressively using pesticides, our crop yields have actually decreased. I ask these intellectuals to imagine a world in which farmers paid the same people who pick our produce to also pick crop pests, like a second harvest. A world where industrial pesticides, and their detrimental effects on the environment, are fast becoming obsolete. And in their place, a whole new addition to our culinary landscape.

The presentation portion over, everyone gets down to the serious business of eating, of sampling these new flavors they've come so far to try. I am glad to see my tamales disappearing; since there are more people than tamales, people are even sharing so that everyone gets a taste. After giving them a few minutes to digest the idea, I begin wandering around to the various tables to ask people what they think. Almost everyone agrees the tamales were, at the very least, tasty.

"They certainly weren't any worse than regular tamales," one discerning person said. "I don't know if I'd go so far as to say they were better, but they weren't worse."

"Yeah, if they were similarly priced, I'd consider ordering them at a restaurant."

I take that as a compliment.

"They were excellent," says another guest. "They were my favorite food of the night."

I'm particularly interested in what people think of the idea of bringing food pests to the table. Their reactions to this are mixed.

"I love the idea," says John Openshaw, a medical doctor who researches infectious diseases. "I think it's ahead of its time. But I think it will have its time."

"'Corn earworm' is a terrible name," puts in Paul Hsu. "Maybe use their Latin name." *Heliothis zea* tamales. Heliotamale?

"Also, 'pest' has bad connotations," adds food blogger Rory Everitt. "Maybe make it into a symbol of purity, like they did with mezcal worms. It's going beyond just farm-to-table, it's like bringing the whole ecosystem to the table."

Interesting.

"I liked the novelty of it. Something different, something that has a social-good factor. You're doing something good for yourself and the environment. It's a win-win," someone else adds, chewing thoughtfully.

Why don't we eat insects anymore? What caused the big "bug breakup"?

No one knows for certain why we stopped eating bugs in

the West; however, there are a lot of theories: the Bible, agriculture, climate, and cultural domination. Each makes sense on its own, but the answer is more likely a culmination of all of them.

Recently, I gave a demonstration at Ripley's Believe It or Not! Museum in San Francisco, where I fried up a bunch of crickets. For eating a certain number of them, folks could get a discount to the museum (and a nice free snack). A couple of kids wandered up to the table and looked longingly at the fried crickets on sticks, available with or without "bee vomit."* I asked them if they wanted to try some.

"We really want to, but we can't because they aren't kosher," they said. "Our dad's a rabbi."

"Really," I said, clamping my eyes on Dad, standing a distance away, amused. "Well, that depends on your interpretation of the Torah. Leviticus says that certain insects with legs above their bodies, like grasshoppers or crickets, are okay."

Dad squinted at me. "Where does it say that?"

"Leviticus 11:22."

We all waited while he looked it up on his iPhone.

"Well, I'll be darned," he said.

The kids loved their crickets, and Dad loved the discount. No Jew jokes.

Rabbi Dr. Ari Zivotofsky and his friend Dr. Ari Greenspan have been known to serve locusts at kosher restaurants in Israel, where patrons pay $50 a head to eat like their ancestors did.

Dr. Zivotofsky teaches neuroscience at Bar-Ilan University in Israel. Though he doesn't practice, his rabbinical degree en-

---

* A.k.a. honey.

riches the hobby he shares with Dr. Greenspan, a dentist in Jerusalem—bringing ancient culture to life.

"There used to be Jews all over Europe," Dr. Zivotofsky tells me over Skype, in a voice strikingly like that of Mel Brooks's character Yogurt in *Spaceballs*. "Now they are mainly in Israel and the US. Ari and I try to preserve all that culture that's been lost as a result."

One of these lost aspects of culture is the eating of locusts.

"There was an old Yemenite man who told me that when the locusts swarmed, everyone would get depressed, except the Jewish kids. The Jews at that time were city-dwellers: goldsmiths, blacksmiths, etc., and had no farmland, no crops to lose. The Jewish kids weren't upset at all. They just grabbed their nets and got ready to catch some snacks."

Dr. Zivotofsky tells me of a Yemenite couple whom he and Dr. Greenspan had brought in to help cook one of their popular Masorah ("traditional") dinners. At the sight of the locusts, he says, "She and her husband were salivating. They couldn't wait to eat them."

Dr. Zivotofsky believes that locusts went out of style as a food item simply because of dearth of availability. "You just didn't see them anymore. A girl I met, who'd grown up in Yemen, had lost her taste for them over her lifetime, just because the culture she'd been in didn't offer them. They'd grown strange to her."

Basically, Dr. Zivotofsky confirmed that, again, the main reason we don't eat insects is because that's just not what we do. That's what culture is: a group identity based on beliefs, traditions, and habits. Some of them make sense. Some of them don't. Some of them just are. Our habit of not eating insects is just that, a habit. A habit based on a belief based on our history, a history that has lost the habit of eating insects.

But unfamiliarity doesn't directly explain how we came to have such a strong and abiding disgust for the idea of eating them. As Paul Rozin, the world's leading expert on disgust, noted, we tend to have more disgust regarding animals, yet the idea of eating part of a large African snake would probably not hold the same degree of disgust for most people, despite its comparable proximity to the ground.

The Bible doesn't say much about bugs, but what it does say is pretty clear: that eating certain insects is an abomination (along with haircuts, wearing mixed fibers, and tattoos). Much of what we know as the Bible was adapted from the Torah, and that's where a lot of these abominations were born, so let's start there.

Through observation, the early Torah scribes may have noticed that lobsters and crabs, for instance, are scavengers (think mer-vultures), and that pigs spend an awful lot of time either in their own excrement or in visually similar conditions. Bugs are an easy one. They clearly show up in dirty (read: biologically fecund) conditions, and they live close to the ground. If the whole point of religion is to elevate ourselves above our animalistic brethren, then we can't go around ingesting things that crawl around on the earth, can we? Kind of defeats the whole purpose. Also, some of those bugs eat poop or decaying flesh. So let's make it simple: Only the bugs with "legs up above their bodies" can be eaten:

> Yet among the winged insects that go on all fours you may eat those that have jointed legs above their feet, with which to hop on the ground. Of them you may eat: the locust of any kind, the bald locust of any kind, the cricket of any kind, and the grasshopper of any kind. (Leviticus 11:20–23)

You'll note that eating these insects (locusts, crickets, and grasshoppers, depending on your translation) is quite clearly permitted, while eating shellfish is not:

> Everything in the waters that does not have fins and scales is detestable to you. (Leviticus 11:12)

That "leaping insects" make the cut may have been for various reasons. First, eating them was already established in the culture, and they were an important source of food during swarm season. In fact, according to a certain interpretation, following the locust installment of the ten plagues, the Egyptians "rejoiced and said 'Let us gather them and fill our barrels with them.'" Pickling was a popular method of preservation, and it's likely that would have been the intention.

God replied, "Wicked people, with the plague that I have brought against you, are you going to rejoice?!" and immediately brought upon them a western wind and blew the remaining locusts into the Red Sea, leaving none for the Egyptians to recoup their losses by eating.

Beyond locusts, though, insects in general were off the cultural menu during biblical times. Although most of the other foods have made it back on to the menu, like pork and shellfish, for instance (for Bible readers, at least), bugs stayed taboo.

Why? Well, it's possible a culture of disgust became associated with them. As civilization expanded and solidified, the only time people may have really encountered bugs was when they infiltrated a "human" space: a home or agricultural area.

But isn't that rational? I can hear you asking. *Insects spread disease, don't they?*

Yes and no. First of all, it's important to consider the vast biological differences between you and, say, a grasshopper. The grasshopper is so fundamentally, biologically different from you, and from any other mammal, that any pathogens that attack the grasshopper are highly unlikely to also attack a human. Swine flu, avian flu, mad cow disease—there are no insect equivalents of these. Grasshoppers are cold-blooded, have their skeletons on the outside of their bodies, and have open circulatory systems, which means their blood flows back and forth through their body outside of blood vessels. They even have green blood. Anatomically speaking, they are practically nothing like a human.

The insects that spread human diseases, like mosquitoes, do so by transferring diseased human blood between humans. A mosquito is not affected by malaria. A cockroach isn't affected by the germs it walks through and thus spreads to other areas. An urban cockroach that has been who-knows-where is not the type I'm advising you to eat. Quite the opposite.

The bottom line is that wild insects can indeed move diseases from one place to another, especially within heavily human-populated areas. A virus can be airborne, but air isn't bad in general. In fact, airplanes are one of the most effective vectors of disease, but no one denigrates them as a whole. Insects themselves are not especially prone to diseases, nor are they particular magnets for disease. Certain species of insect occasionally become embroiled in human messes, just as rodents and even livestock can.

There is the potential danger of parasites—certain parasites that affect insects can also affect people, just like the parasites in any other kind of meat can. Cooking is the main way this is handled. If an insect is properly cooked, so would be any stowaways. If an insect is farmed, the likelihood that it contains a parasite at all goes way down.

For the first time in my life, I began growing food in my own garden this year. The tomatoes, garlic, and herbs did fine, but my beloved kale was constantly besieged by "plant lice": aphids.

Now, I've thought, read, and written a great deal about insects. I know these aphids are sap-suckers, little more than leaf mosquitoes. They have a better diet than most vegans: All they do is suck kale blood. Basically, they're on a constant green-juice cleanse. They turn this kale blood into animal tissue, making them, in reality, little hyperconcentrated kale nuggets. Not only that, but new studies have found they, unlike any other animal on Earth, can actually photosynthesize. Chia seeds and quinoa take a nutritional backseat to these little pellets of post-kale product. They make the nutrients available in kale even more bioavailable, since there's no cellulose to break down.

But man, they *piss me off.*

The anger that subsistence farmers must feel toward the invasions of insects must be exponentially bigger and deeper than my almost satisfying dalliance with the aphids. It must be, in fact, huge enough to pervade an entire culture. In this sense, agriculture in general may be another big part of the answer to "Why don't Westerners eat bugs?"

The truth is that agriculture is a fairly new concept to our species—ants, for instance, have been doing it for millennia. Ants farm aphids for their sugary secretions and grow fungus inside their ant tunnels. Humans have existed and eaten for millions of years, but we've only practiced agriculture in a widespread way for the last ten thousand. This comparatively thin chapter of human history now pervades the majority of our cultures. Planting vegetables in the ground has been a way for us to more closely guarantee, or control, our survival. By having a steady stream of calories, we've been able to stay put long enough to advance technologically.

As with all progress, there are good and bad consequences. Agriculture seems as obvious, necessary, and God-given as the Garden of Eden. But it's not necessarily a perfect system.

In order to grow food plants, we must first "clear the land." Now, the term "clear the land" is reminiscent of my clearing my kale leaves of aphids: It seems natural, good, clean, necessary. You clear the land of "unhelpful" and "inedible" elements like trees, brush, and other native growth. You also clear decaying matter: leaves, wood, and so on. The other things you clear are the animals that might interfere or compete with you for your crops: rodents, bugs, bigger game like deer perhaps. What seems as clear and correct as cleaning house is actually a rather large and potentially irreversible disruption of a naturally occurring, carefully evolved, and balanced ecosystem in favor of a monospecies. The monospecies is the crop we're intending to grow.

But what about those cultures that don't harbor these antibug feelings? Were they just so desperate for food that they had to get over it, literally swallow their hatred and fear for lack of calories?

This seems a bit unlikely. Farmers in vastly different places and cultures have actually fetched higher market prices for the pests that feed on their crops than the crops themselves. So what's the difference? Why can a Thai or African farmer stomach the idea of bringing their crop pests to market rather than eliminating them entirely? Why would Native Americans eat locusts when they swarm, while American pioneers eschewed them entirely?

Why are we so different from these seemingly more nature-connected cultures?

Take a moment and consider why you yourself don't eat bugs. They're dirty, right? Disease-ridden? From the dirt and muck of the world? Potentially poisonous? Teeming? Squirmy, crawly? Is there an anger there, a feeling like they just shouldn't exist, as if they are a mere cross to bear for being alive? A nuisance, something to "take care of"?

I've talked about these questions with many people over the years: paleontologists, anthropologists, entomologists. Every year or so, several of us entomophagy enthusiasts gather at an event and try to get to the bottom of it.

From everything I've read and pieced together over the years, the answer has to do with climate. If you look at the existing humans and apes that do eat insects, many of their societies are located in areas where free-ranging New World monkeys live or lived. In other words, tropical climes. There's a reason bugs grow bigger in places like Texas and Florida — heat. Remember how insects are cold-blooded? Well, in warmer, moister climates, they are more active, more reproductive, and bigger. Show me a place where the bugs get big and plentiful enough to make a meal, and I'll show you a culture that accepts them. Unless, of course, their values have been influenced by Europeans.

Generally speaking, the closer you get to the equator, the more likely it is that a culture will have some strain of insect consumption. Latin and South America, Africa, Asia — these are all places where entomophagy is most prevalent. Granted, not in every country, but it's a heck of a lot more common than it is in, say, Russia, Sweden, or Canada.

In Mexico, more than 500 species of edible insects have been recorded.* In Australia, witchetty grubs and honeypot ants are still eaten by Aborigines. In Africa, people are still getting busted for trying to smuggle out kilos of highly valuable mopane worms to Africans living in places like Britain or Switzerland. Across Asia, terrestrial invertebrates like palm grubs, crickets, grasshoppers, bamboo worms, scorpions, and more are eaten with more or less regularity. Basically, you can divide the planet into bug-eaters and non-bug-eaters. And climate has everything to do with it.

But what about here in the States? Native American tribes, depending on their region, were all about eating insects. During the Dust Bowl era, while pioneers battled locusts,[†] the Utah Paiutes stockpiled salted, dried grasshoppers as protection against future famine.

"Ironically what the native Americans . . . regarded as food provided by their gods, the white settlers regarded as a plague, which they prayed to their God to destroy," writes Ronald Taylor in *Butterflies in My Stomach: Or, Insects as Human Nutrition.*

As recently as a few decades ago, there were still conflicts between the Paiute Indians of Mono Lake and the park

---

* This number was calculated through the efforts of biologist Julieta Ramos-Elorduy, author of *Creepy Crawly Cuisine* and countless papers and studies on the subject of entomophagy in her native Mexico.

† Locusts are different from grasshoppers in that when they sense the presence of too many other locusts, they morph both physically and "psychologically," going from solitary, quiet creatures to hypersocial, teeming, buffed-out versions of their former selves. It's as if you gave an introvert Adderall and steroids at the same time.

rangers over pandora pine moth caterpillar rights. The Paiutes wanted to eat the caterpillars, and the rangers wanted to
kill them with insecticides to protect the pine trees they were
feeding on. The Paiutes didn't want to ingest insecticide, nor
did they want to give up their traditional food. Sadly, over the
years, they largely have.

So what happened? Why don't we eat insects in our fancy
restaurants, like they do in Mexico City, Thailand, and China?

The answer is that, culturally speaking, we are of European, not Native American descent. We may have learned
how to farm certain crops from the Native Americans, but we
never took on what was then seen as the "savage" practice of
eating insects.

Speaking of things we got from Native Americans, the
original Thanksgiving table would likely have included plenty
of seafood: lobster, salmon, oysters. While these foods are considered delicacies today, at that point in time, they were considered a poor man's fare at best. It was an embarrassment for
the Pilgrims to have to serve lobster (which at that point piled
up on the beaches after a storm) to their guests. Shellfish, like
oysters and clams, were ground up for pig feed as recently
as the 1800s. Bluefin tuna, today the most sought-after, expensive fish on the market, until the 1960s was either *thrown
away* or turned into cat food. Sportfishers liked to catch them
because of their impressive size, but after taking a picture with
their catch, they would pay someone to drag it away and bury
it. It wasn't until a Japanese businessman from Japan Airlines,
searching for cargo to pack on return flights to Tokyo, began
importing bluefin that it became valuable—and then only to
the Japanese, who had developed a taste for it in sushi.

Eating sushi is actually not that different from eating insects. Thirty years ago, going out for sushi in places like San

Francisco and Los Angeles was still considered edgy and made some people queasy. Now you can find sushi joints in Nebraska.

As Trevor Corson explains it in his book *The Story of Sushi*, sushi worked here in the States for three reasons: one, the USDA announced that fish was healthy; two, the TV movie *Shogun* came out, causing a wave of Japanophilia; and three, it was a party food. The culture of visiting a sushi restaurant became part of the appeal: The chefs would yell when you came in, wave their Ginsu knives about, and serve you something challenging and brightly colored to eat, while refilling your cup with sake till you didn't care what was on your plate anymore. It was a story you could tell your friends. If they'd had iPhones back in the '80s, Instagram would've been even more flooded with sushi pics than it is now.

Edible insects could be approaching just such a trifecta to crest the wave. In today's increasingly eco-conscious climate, they are being touted as a highly sustainable food source; they are highly cultural and unique—perfect fodder for the growing foodie population; and they're nutritious in an age when nearly everything on the menu comes with its share of ethical conflict.

There's a scene in the popular TV show *Portlandia* that features two Portland restaurant patrons, Peter and Nance, who have some questions about the chicken.

The waitress begins by saying, "The chicken is a heritage breed, woodland raised, on a diet of sheep's milk, soy, and hazelnuts—"

Peter interrupts to ask, "And is this local?"

"Yes, absolutely," says the waitress.

"I'm going to ask you just one more time," says Peter, like an Israeli TSA agent. "It is local?"

"It is," says the waitress.

"And is it USDA organic, Oregon organic, Portland organic . . . ?" Nance scrutinizes.

"It's just all-across-the-board, organic," assures the waitress, who excuses herself and comes back with the chicken's papers. His* name was Collin. He was a Rhode Island Red. He had four acres on a rural farm through which to roam free.

Peter inquires into Collin's social life—was he happy? Popular amongst the other chickens?

In the end, none of the waitress' answers are enough to satisfy Peter and Nance, who leave the restaurant and drive the 30 miles to the farm to check out Collin's pre-menu environs before being willing to order him.

This parody might be over the top, but honestly, it's not off by much. Just what constitutes ethical meat has become very narrowly defined. Insects fit into these tight parameters quite comfortably.

---

* In real life, the chicken would not be a "he." Nor would "he" drink sheep's milk.

6

Learning How to Taste

THERE ARE NEARLY nineteen hundred recorded edible insect species on Earth and counting. How many different types of meat have you sampled in your lifetime? Most people never go beyond the standard dozen-plus basics of chicken, beef, pork, lamb, and maybe five to ten kinds of fish. Compared with the 500 varieties of insect eaten in Mexico alone, this is a fairly limited flavor palate—the "beginner box" of culinary Crayolas.

Insects represent the majority of the animal biomass on Earth. They have thousands of different habitats, and many species have evolved to eat a single type of plant. Considering all the different plants and ecosystems there are, and their corresponding insect populations, this opens up a kaleidoscope of flavors.

In general, insects tend to taste a bit nutty, especially when roasted. This comes from the natural fats they contain, combined with the crunchiness of their mineral-rich exoskeletons. Crickets, for instance, taste like nutty shrimp, whereas most larvae I've tried have a nutty mushroom flavor. My two favorites, wax moth caterpillars (a.k.a. wax worms) and bee larvae, taste like enoki–pine nut and bacon-chanterelle, respectively.

Recently, when I served this grub at the LA Natural History Museum's Bug Fair Cook-Off,* one kid on the judging panel said my "Alice in Wonderland" dish of sautéed wax worms and oyster mushrooms tasted like macaroni and cheese, while the rest agreed that my Bee-LT Sandwich tasted like it was made with real bacon.

The term "bug" has a specific taxonomic meaning, indicating an insect of the order Hemiptera, known as the "true bugs," and includes cicadas, aphids, plant hoppers, leafhoppers, shield bugs, and others. It is also widely used by non-entomologists as an umbrella term covering land arthropods in general, including arachnids like scorpions and spiders.

Having established that arachnids are included in our general discussion of entomophagy, their tastes should be included as well. In my experience, arachnids often taste like a light, earthy version of shellfish, crab, and lobster in particular. This makes sense since, from a biological standpoint, bugs and crustaceans are quite closely related. However, the air-breathing group of these invertebrates has one distinct advantage over its sea-steeped brethren: They aren't bottom-feeders. Scorpions, tarantulas, and other edible arachnids all catch their prey live, unlike crabs, which are just as happy to feast on detritus.

These examples are fairly tame and recognizable; most people can swallow the idea of nutty mushrooms and earthy shellfish. But there are also flavors in the bug world that can

---

* I lost to David George Gordon's delicious orthopteran stir-fry.

hardly be equated with anything familiar to most Westerners. The taste of giant water bug practically defies description; as one writer enthused after his first time eating them, "There is simply nothing in the annals of our culture to which I can direct your attention that would hint at the nature of [its] flavor."

When fresh, these aggressive beetles have a scent like a crisp green apple. Large enough to yield tiny fillets, they taste like anchovies soaked in banana-rose brine, with the consistency of a light, flaky fish. Dave Gracer likes to serve tiny filaments of their flesh atop cubes of watermelon, and even this minuscule amount of the bug is enough to infuse an entire mouthful. It's no wonder their extract is a common ingredient in Thai sauces.

Conservative eaters are likely to prefer to stick to what they know, but if you're anything like me, you'll find this galaxy of mysterious new flavors simply too compelling to resist. Indeed, some of the world's top gastronauts have begun to explore it in earnest.

Noma is the much-buzzed-about restaurant in Copenhagen, Denmark, that beat out elBulli for *Restaurant* magazine's best restaurant in the world award in 2010 and has managed to hold on to the title for three years running. A tiny place on the waterfront edge of an old stone maritime warehouse, the restaurant's trappings are so subtle you'd miss it if you weren't really looking. Yet Noma turned down close to a million would-be diners in the last year alone. From its windows, the city skyline, with its slender church spires and geometric modern architecture, is silhouetted so beautifully in the pinkening sunset that famous head chef René Redzepi comes out to snap a quick photo, then ducks back in before becoming the subject of photos himself. Redzepi was recently named one of *Time* magazine's World's 100 Most Influential People.

Ten years ago, Copenhagen was virtually unknown as far as food went, a "culinary backwater," as Michael Booth called it in *Copenhagen Encounter*. In other words, no one went to Denmark for the food, unless they had a hankering for reindeer meat. Today people fly from all over the world to sample aspects of the fiercely home-proud food movement that has flourished here, known as the New Nordic Cuisine, largely established by Redzepi and his Noma cofounder, Claus Meyer.

Redzepi's perspective on the New Nordic Cuisine has extended its tentacles to gourmets around the world as chefs strive to imitate his style, for which intrepid diners pay $400 apiece to eat things like fried reindeer moss, hay ash, twigs, ants and seaweed. This may sound like the world's biggest rip-off, but the idea is that one is eating, well, ideas taken from nature, refined through art and tradition, and re-presented as nature on the plate.

"The flavors at Noma are intense. They're not for everyone," Daniel Giusti, the former chef of 1789 in Washington, DC, now a soldier in Redzepi's army, told the *Washington Post*. "There's an aura about this restaurant that I've never seen before. René can do anything he wants."

The New Nordic Cuisine is about the fusion of immediacy and history at once. It's about what is available locally, seasonally, and, generally, in abundance—the here and now of nutrient sources. It's also about the identity of a place, both naturally and culturally. In the Nordic region—which comprises Denmark, Finland, Iceland, Norway, Sweden, the Faroe Islands, Greenland, Svalbard, and Åland—food preservation techniques like fermenting and pickling have been popular for centuries, likely because of the percentage of the year spent in cold, dark winter. Food has to last, to warm, to nourish deeply—but also to inspire and invigorate during the long, lightless months. Ingredients can be extended but also intensified through the application of salt, yeasts, mold, and time.

This is all the easier to grasp now in the beginning of November, when it's already so cold I have to wear two jackets, gloves, and a thick hat at all times. I'm here in Copenhagen to visit Nordic Food Lab (NFL), the R&D branch of Noma.

Taking humble ingredients and elevating them to a lofty status is Redzepi's proven specialty. In early 2012, he posed the question: If he could serve bark, branches, weeds, and other dubiously edible ingredients at Noma, why couldn't he serve the humblest ingredient of all—insects?

He tasked NFL, the nonprofit institute he established and then dedicated to searching and stretching the boundaries of edibility, with discovering the answer. Since then, they've been experimenting with various species, trying to find the most delicious ways of presenting ingredients viewed as nonedible by the public.

Docked just across the cold black canal is NFL's floating houseboat of a home. Like Noma, it has an unassuming exterior—a small gray boat surrounded by bicycles. Much has been written about the relatively small expanse bracketed by Noma and NFL. But no one has written about their foray into edible insects.

I show up bright and early in the chilly rain. The boat looks cozy and inviting, with its squares of warm yellow glass gleaming against the gray; a clean, well-lighted place for cooks. I make it onto the boat's front porch, where I hover in front of the glass doors and wave.

A handful of edgily stylish, serious-looking men, each with his own air of focused intensity, ushers me inside. There's somber Michael Bom Frost, who splits his time between being director of NFL and director of studies for the Gastronomy and Health program at Copenhagen University. Next is animated Scotsman Benedict Reade, the new head of culinary research and development, followed by stoic, tattooed Lars Williams, Ben's predecessor and current R&D director at Noma, and keen-eyed Josh Evans, an intern from Yale Sustainable Food Project. These guys help dream up and then test some of the most innovative food ideas in the world. I peel off my wet layers in the warmth of the space, which is spare yet welcoming like many Danish interiors. The room is part designer kitchen, part laboratory, part casually elegant meeting space. Stacks of beakers and flasks coexist with pots and pans. Containers holding various colors and consistencies have labels like BEETS, BREAD YEAST 11/09 and SORREL, RED WINE, BARLEY MOLD 02/07. It looks like exactly what it is: a preternaturally hip foodie think tank.

Someone offers me coffee. I'd already decided to say yes to anything I'm offered here, and coffee's obviously a no-brainer. I am handed it black, in a lovely little handmade cup. No mention of cream or sugar is made—everyone's drinking theirs straight. I take a sip. It's fantastic. Later, I'll be very glad I had it—it revved my brain for the daylong conversation about food I was about to have with some of the world's foremost thinkers on the subject. NFL is a team of people passionate about exploring and expressing ideas, be it through food or words.

I ask them what they think of the idea that insects are the food of the future.

"Well, if any one thing becomes the food of the future,

that's a very depressing future," says Ben Reade in his charm-
ing brogue. "We need diversity, and that's why we're interested in looking at insects—it's another walk of life that we
can investigate. We have the whole phylogenetic tree that
we can eat, so we have to look at all the different branches. I
think it's really important to make sure people realize that insects are another ingredient that can be added to a repertoire,
and not suddenly become *the* ingredient, when there is no *the*
ingredient, is there? That's only an economist's way of looking at things. And if economists look at food too much, then
things get dangerous."

"The same thing happened with soybeans, right?" adds researcher Josh Evans. "Soybeans have been used for hundreds
of thousands of years in many cultures, and they're perfectly
healthy if they're prepared the right way. But once they were
touted as *the* ingredient that everyone will consume, that will
save the world, that's when vast swathes of the Amazon were
cut down."

"We see insects not as *the* food of the future but as an interesting addition to the foods we already have," says Michael
Bom Frost, whose background is in sensory science (whatever *that* means). "To convince Europe to eat insects, it's not
enough to fry them up or to extract the protein. I think we
have to lower the barriers for first-time entomophagists. If you
just hand someone a cricket, and say, 'Eat it!' I think there's a
ninety-nine percent chance of rejection. But if you give them
something that's really delicious, that's in a familiar setting,
I think we can lower the outright rejection rate a lot. And I
think that's really important because then we can start building on it."

Michael offers Singapore as an example, where they are using a water filtration system to treat and reuse the water from

the sewers. If you think about it, they're drinking shit water, but the truth is it's perfectly safe to drink. On the one hand, there is disgust, but on the other, there is a societal need that must be addressed.

"We want to address this need with deliciousness as the vehicle for promoting insects, and not saying, 'Eat this because it's good for the environment,' or 'because it's healthy protein,' but 'because it tastes good,'" says Michael.

The term "deliciousness" is bandied about with great seriousness here at NFL, and we discuss how this mouth-first approach applies to eating insects—asking first, "How does it taste?" instead of "What is it?" Nothing edible should be considered off-limits just because of our prejudices about it.

"No *ideas* are inherently disgusting. That's food fascism," says Ben.

Michael, Josh, and I head out to the seashore to forage for periwinkle sea snails, shrimp, and "strand hoppers," which are essentially sand fleas. *Strand* is Danish for beach. We'll be fishing for aquatic invertebrates.

On the way over, I learn what it means to be a food sensory scientist. What Michael does is scientifically interpret taste tests, usually to help develop healthier products that still taste good. One of his most notable accomplishments was coming up with data suggesting that 0.5 percent fat in milk was the lowest amount necessary for consumers to feel satisfaction. Today, that category makes up 40 percent of milk sales in Denmark.

"It's about finding a sweet spot between health and good taste in a common food," says Michael with a twinkle in his eye. It's clear he is passionate about what he does.

The sparse, beautiful beach scene blows me away. The glassy waves of the Øresund Strait lap gently on the shore of

Amager Strand, an artificial island added by the city in 2005, which can be reached by metro. Wave-tangled, multicolored ribbons of seaweed line the sand, like the streamers of a wild, forgotten birthday party. It's almost winter, so there won't be any parties here today; it's about 40 degrees even in the intermittent sun. The only other people out here are a few locals walking their dogs.

Michael and Josh laughingly pull on their giant army-green waders, bought especially for the occasion. I ask how cold the water is, if people go swimming here in the summertime. I try to picture the empty beach full of people and noise, where now there's just wind and sand.

"People go swimming here all year round," says Josh. "Crazy Danes."

They gather up their nets: one giant, practically person-sized one for Michael, a smaller green one for Josh. They step into the waves and march out into the water, soon up to their hips in the chilly Øresund. The water is clear, so they can hone in on their tiny prey.

The ocean is a choppy slate-blue extension of the sky, through which billowy mountain ranges of cloud patterns pass. Denmark is big-sky country. The light changes every few minutes, and I snap madly away at the scene of the two epicurean fishermen/academics, caught between sea and sky as they collect ingredients from the blue expanse. A line of white wind turbines in the background completes the scene, as well as part of the context: Copenhagen aims to be the world's first carbon-neutral city by 2025. Crazy Danes, indeed.

"How is it out there?" I call. They've gone quite a ways out, insulated by the thick rubber and unimpeded by the smooth waves. They wave back, grinning.

Michael is the first to wade back in with his catch. He

kneels down and shakes clumps of olive-green bladder wrack into a bucket. Sea snails, shrimp, and tiny, darting strand hoppers fall out.

Context, Michael and Josh say, is as important as the ingredients on the plate. Taste, woven with philosophy and shot through with science, seems to be the conversational culture of this team, members of which must be as steeped in this sort of rhetoric as their weeds are in fermenting brew.

"People eating food is the only way they get the full experience," Michael says.

"In the same way that there's no such thing as a painting without the context of the painting—even in the most modernistic of galleries, it's still a white wall," says Josh. "There's still a texture, there's still lighting, there's still a mood that's created. There's no such thing as a taste without a context."

The sea air bites at our cheeks, the wind flaps through our hair. The waves curl under, collapsing gently against the sand. Jellyfish nestled in masses of seaweed rock forward and back under the clear, undulating surface of the water. The clouds are piled high, slow as migrating herds across the wide blue sky. Josh runs down the beach and comes back with an armful of treasure: beach mustard. I grab a purple-flowered stalk and take a bite. It's just like a delicate broccoli, salted by the sea air.

Michael fishes out a nearly transparent, gangly shrimp from the bucket's brine. Like Lisa Simpson said, they aren't really that much different from grasshoppers.

"Noma currently serves a live shrimp on ice with a brown butter emulsion, and for that, people are like, *whoa*," says Josh. "It's still sort of at the frontier of what's seen as acceptable. Or even delicious."

"We can eat them alive and pretend we're at Noma," says Michael.

I find I have no qualms about putting the live shrimp in my mouth, especially in this context. I wasn't worried about hurting it—it would be crushed instantly between my teeth, as good a death as any it might encounter living in the wild. I recalled something Redzepi had said about these live shrimp: "The taste of these shrimp changes from day to day, depending on the conditions of the ocean. Eating them is really like tasting the ocean on that day."

Today the ocean tastes sweet, and tender, and fresh, with a subtle brightness that is hard to qualify. Maybe this is what the Japanese are on about, with their super-fresh food and live sushi.

Back at the lab, we boil up the sea snails we collected. Josh leads me on an appetizer journey around the kitchen. First I try the fermented grasshopper garum that tastes like fish sauce in its complexity and emphasizes the umami flavor of many insects. Then I taste the bee-larvae granola he's made for a breakfast event they're holding next week. It's crunchy and creamy and savory at once. Delicious.

The sea snails cook up quickly and are light, fresh, and chewy, like an extra-firm shrimp. As with all the other invertebrate morsels I've tried here, there certainly isn't anything off-putting about them. Quite the opposite, in fact. If you didn't know they were insects and snails, you'd never question them. Slap a fancy title on them, like they did with Chilean sea bass (a.k.a. Patagonian toothfish), put them on the menu at an upscale restaurant, and people would order them.

I leave before dinner at Noma (the restaurant books up months in advance), but the conversation during my day at

NFL alone will keep me going for quite a while. Sometimes ideas are nourishment enough.

As it turns out, a sniffle I'd felt before leaving for my day with the food scholars blossomed into a cold after all that time on the freezing beach. At this point I'd been on a madcap research dash around chilly Europe for over a week, in my holey hiking shoes (note to self, *never* go to Europe past October without a warm and cool-looking pair of boots), cotton knit hat, and mid-temp poly-fill jacket (they wear animal products in Denmark for a reason).

It was a pretty bad cold, actually, the kind you can't will yourself out of, even when you're trading a day in one of the most beautiful and exciting cities in the world for one spent huddled under the covers watching reruns of old shows that aren't even shown anymore in America. Meanwhile, exotic yet deeply homey foods waited around every corner, and I was missing all of them. Foods from a hobbit's hearth: reindeer stew; cream of local, foraged mushroom; bright red sausages with pickles; elderflower juice.

I couldn't eat them anyway, not at the rate at which my body was converting fluids to mucus. All I wanted was soup—and not some heavy, winey, reduced-to-a-gravy reindeer stew. Just something light and brothy that I could sip till I got warm inside. Brian, my husband, suggested we go to the supermarket, see what we could find, and make ourselves some homemade soup.

"What, like we do at home?"

"Why not?" We were staying in a place with a kitchen, after all. The idea of peeling and cutting and chopping wasn't exactly appealing, but as the sun sank lower and temperatures dropped, I knew my options were slimming. My stomach rumbled. It was this or straight rye *brood* (bread).

We headed down to the corner supermarket, the kind found throughout Copenhagen. This particular one advertised a special out front before you entered the store: fill a paper bag with root vegetables from the featured bins for 25 krones, or about $4. Amazed, we filled ours with pink and purple beets, small golden onions, white parsnips and turnips, and purple, yellow, white, and orange carrots. We grabbed some garlic, ginger, and bouillon inside, and brought our rooty, rainbow bounty home. Brian thought to add in bits of the salami we'd brought with us as a snack from Amsterdam. We peeled and chopped and boiled and simmered, and soon had one of the tastiest soups I'd ever had. It was sharp and hearty and brothy and full of vitamins. I couldn't get enough.

The next day, we went back and refilled our paper bag with these, the cheapest, most seasonal available ingredients, the multicolored root vegetables of pre-winter Nordic lands. After a couple of days of this vitamin A–rich farmer's brew, I was finally well enough to take in an actual meal at a restaurant. Perhaps one run by a chef who'd trained under Redzepi and then gone on to open his own restaurant. We decided on Manfreds after it was recommended to us three times, all by different sources: the inflight magazine, our Airbnb host, and the tribe at NFL.

We ordered the prix fixe, rubbing our hands together in anticipation of a fancy meal at last. The food did not disappoint: warm beet salad with smoky, creamy local cheese; barely cooked turnips with sorrel sauce, reminiscent of apple slices with lemon, only savory; roasted carrots with pickled onions; smashed parsnips with unidentifiable but delicious

julienned greens; crispy fried pork with herbs. A truly memorable meal with enough detail and surprise that each dish war-
ranted discussion and dissection, like a chapter in a book.

Then I realized that we had just eaten a different version
of the same raw ingredients we'd bought at the market. The
dinner was at heart a succession of root dishes, the same ones
we'd simmered in our humble, borrowed pot. Beets, turnips,
carrots, parsnips, pork. The essence of fall. The cheapest,
most available and abundant ingredients. In our own, uncon-
scious way, we'd produced the New/Old Nordic Cuisine right
in our rented apartment kitchen, and it had strengthened me
to experience the arc to its finish, this high-end expression of
simple farmer's food. Perhaps helped by the natural wine we'd
been drinking along with the meal, accompanied by my recently broken fever, I found myself enraptured in a moment
of spirituality. It was like walking the trail of a pilgrimage for
the photographs and accidentally having a holy experience of
your own.

It was a perfect last night in Copenhagen, and considering
what I had learned about food from a firsthand perspective,
almost magical. I can't wait to go back . . . in July, maybe.

7

In the Mouth of the Beholder

I'M IN TOKYO, and I'm late.

There's an old saying in Japan: If you're not twenty minutes early to an appointment, you're late. Well, I'm *actually* late, about fifteen minutes or so, which means to the Japanese people waiting for me, it might as well be the next day. I confused the Nishi-Magome and Magome Stations, got off the express train a stop early, and now have to wait for the slower, local train.

I grew up partly in Tokyo. When I was nine years old, my dad's company opened a branch there, so my whole family moved over. Despite the fact that the spidery symbols on the subway signs were skittering back into my head with surprising familiarity, I'd still made a fatal mistake. Not only was I going to be late, but I was going to be late meeting an old classmate from Tokyo grade school, Mikiko Baba, whom I had convinced to join me at a fancy bug party.

Mikiko had agreed to be my translator at this bug-cooking gathering. She warned me that she didn't even like looking at bugs, blinking her eyes upward when I tried to show her some pictures on my phone of things we might be eating.

"Okay, okay," she said, waving her hand as if to swat them away. "Let's just go."

The gathering of the Tokyo Bug-Eating Club has taken place monthly at a little café called Yoru-No-Hirune ("Night Nap") for about six years, making it one of the longest-running and most popular of its kind in the world. It was started by Shoichi Uchiyama, an entomophagy enthusiast and author of two books in Japanese on the subject—one a cookbook and the other a more general treatment of the subject.

Uchiyamasan started his career as an electrical engineer for Fujitsu but felt his true place was, as he puts it, "surrounded by books." A passionate fan of Russian literature, he made his living for many years as a translator. Six years ago, he became friends with Katsuhiko Kadota, the owner of Yoru-No-Hirune, the two united by their love of books and history.

Yoru-No-Hirune is a dark, retro, hip-but-cozy spot that functions as a café during the day, a bar at night, and a library/reading spot always. It is thick with books and atmosphere. Old records line the wood-paneled walls, '60s lounge music grooves on the record player, and a sumo match plays silently on the small TV at the end of the bar. The venue is a delicious mix of ages and cultures, and has an impressive manga (Japanese graphic novels) collection; books in many languages surround the tiny, child-sized chairs and low tables. There's something here for everyone, and a groovy, laid-back vibe to boot.*

Uchiyamasan, whose name means "in the mountains,"

---

* In order to re-create the image in my mind, I've made a Walter Wanderley Pandora station, which I highly recommend.

grew up in the Nagano Prefecture. Nagano is a mountainous region of Japan, historically somewhat cut off from the coastal areas, and is known for its unusual cuisine, especially insects. Residents' penchant for bugs makes sense, if you think about their geography. While coastal parts of Japan got their protein from ocean fish, more central, enclosed areas would have eaten what was available locally. To this day, older residents of Nagano still participate in wasp-hunting parties to make *jibachi senbei,* a rice cookie embedded with wasps.

Uchiyamasan recalls one of the first times he ate insects as a boy growing up in Nagano, which became famous for its sericulture (silkworm farming) and silk reeling. His grandfather was eating *sanagi donburi,* or marinated silkworm pupae over rice.

"Try it," insisted his *ojiisan,* holding out a brown pupa between his chopsticks. "It's good for you."

It wasn't until forty or so years later that his grandfather's words hit home for Uchiyamasan. In the late '90s, he went to an event showcasing the edible insects of global cultures.

"There were pictures of people from Africa, from South America, hunting insects and eating them, enjoying them," he says. The connection to his childhood lit up, and he realized eating insects was a real, global thing, not just some idiosyncratic custom from his hometown.

He and his friends talked it over and then went down to the riverside to catch grasshoppers, which they promptly fried and ate.

"They were *good,*" he says, laughing. "We weren't expecting that."

After that he began experimenting with more recipes. His wife, also from Nagano, helped him perfect them.

"She won't eat the cockroaches, though."

I tell him I understand; I'm not a big fan of eating cockroaches, either.

"Just wait," he says with a smile.

Uchiyamasan and the owner of Yoru-No-Hirune decided to hold an edible insect event at the café. Thirty people showed up to that first meeting. *It's a hit!* they thought, and decided to keep it going. Uchiyamasan advertises the events on his blog and via flyers posted along the Orange Line, which he says "a lot of interesting people ride." Kind of like the L train in New York that shuttles hipsters back and forth between Williamsburg and Manhattan.

The attendees at tonight's party are a mix, equally represented gender-wise, largely younger, but ultimately spanning four decades. There are engineers, students, programmers, car salespeople, biologists, a dental technician, and even a self-defense specialist. There are ripped jeans, short skirts, and even a kimono. Uchiyamasan was once asked in an interview with the blog *Tokyo Scum Brigade:* "If herbivore men are considered passive, and carnivore men are aggressive, then what are insectivore men?"

"They don't have any taboos regarding food and are interested in new things. They place a high premium on healthy living," replied Uchiyamasan.

A very Japanese attitude of cooperation pervades the café and helps to get all the dishes cooked and passed around. My husband gets drafted into helping toast rice balls over an open flame in the alleyway, while I wander around and see what people are up to.

The first bug to make the rounds is *iraga,* a kind of moth larvae, found in tiny, robin's egg–like cocoons. Noborusan, a lanky man in a gorgeous black sweater embroidered with cherry blossoms, holds a small pile of the patterned nuts in his hand and offers them around. He says he found them "in the forest." We crack open the nut-like cocoons with our teeth and eat the larvae raw—living inside the cocoons, their potential exposure to parasites is low. They are delicate, nutty, and slightly sweet. Tiny, soft little treasures sleeping inside the pretty nuts.

Meanwhile, Satchikosan, who's wearing a pink kimono with a spiderweb on the obi, and a friend are off in a corner, making a version of *kuri kinton,* a New Year's treat made ordinarily with *satsumaimo* (Japanese sweet potatoes) and sweet chestnuts. They are skinning and chopping the sweet potatoes and putting them in a boiling pot atop a hotplate. Then Satchikosan turns her attention to a small blue-patterned plate piled with giant water bugs. Using a pair of cooking shears, she expertly slices through their tough exoskeletons, extracting the fragrant meat. When the potatoes are cooked, she mashes them with a little mirin (Japanese sweet cooking wine) and the beetle meat. The two women then form the mixture into little balls, topping them not with the traditional crushed chestnuts, but instead with preserved weaver ant eggs. The finished balls are then put into small paper wrappers and set on a tray. Unable to wait, I manage to finagle one away from them.

I can safely say this is the best insect-based dish I've ever tried. The delicate combination of mirin-seasoned sweet potato with the perfumed hint of beetle essence, topped with the light, fresh, burst-in-your-mouth ant eggs, was something extremely special to experience. Undeniably good, undeniably exotic—and for me, a melt-in-your-mouth melding of my unusual childhood and quirky present.

Next up are pretty pink slices of *kamaboko* (fish cake) with a dollop of seasoned mayonnaise and topped with marinated moths. The moths are salty and chewy, and a decent complement to the mildly fishy chewiness of the fish cake. *Kamaboko,* with its bright, warm festive colors, is eaten around the New Year as a reminder of the symbolism of the Rising Sun. This was followed by roasted grasshoppers covered in cheese, a surprisingly tasty snack that made more sense in the mouth than on the plate.

Outside several people with quiet smiles are standing around a flame toasting *mochi* (pounded rice balls) on sticks. Their conversation rises in murmurs as they watch the flames lick the white rice. Meanwhile, passersby have no idea that these traditional-looking treats will soon be slathered with a sweet miso sauce blended with wasp larvae.

When the sticks are done, everyone takes one and tries it—even Mikiko. This is probably the second-tastiest bug treat I've ever had. The sweet miso with the toasted rice is delightful, complemented by the creamy nuttiness of the wasp larvae.

Jun Mitsuhashi, author of *Edible Insects of the World* (only available in Japanese), wrote that Japanese emperor Hirohito favored a dish made from wasps and rice. While recovering from pancreatic surgery, even if he had no appetite and skipped everything else on his tray, he would often finish the wasps, partly because of their purported medicinal properties.

"The wasp is a protein-rich food and contains B-group vitamins and iron, 10 times as much as ordinary food. For the above reason, it is supposed to stimulate hematopoiesis,"* wrote Mitsuhashi in the November 1988 edition of the *Food Insects Newsletter.* "The old Chineses [*sic*] Pharmacopoeia said that wasps are effective in curing damages to internal organs

---

* The formation of blood cell components.

and in preventing people from getting old when the wasps are administered continuously."

I've tasted dozens of species of insect, prepared many different ways in different regional styles, by chefs from Mexico to the American South to the Netherlands. With great respect to all of them, I've never tasted insects as good as the ones in Japan were. Granted, it could have been my deep familiarity with Japanese food, that little taste of a long-ago home. But the Japanese have a particularly delicate and balanced way of seasoning food and of honoring the essence of the raw ingredients. Even though many of the ingredients were from the same smallish palette of soy-derived sauces, ginger, and wasabi, the tastes were all a bit different and nearly all of them delicious.

Even Mikiko thought so. The woman who couldn't look at a picture of a bug wound up gulping down a silkworm, intensely adorable in her reaction in the way only Japanese women can be (and I should know—I tried hard enough to emulate them while growing up). Good old Mikiko, she even looked cute swallowing a bug.

After the gathering was over, a select few of us (Mikiko had to go off and teach a Pilates class) headed to the next location: a secret party in Aoyama.

This location was as subtly hip as the last. It had an antique *tansu* covered in old turntables; long, low black wooden tables; and a big red bar that overlooked the street via floor-to-ceiling windows. Innocent passersby had no idea what we culinary rebels were up to, here in our secret loft.

This party was a culinary dream come true for me. As we walked in, I saw bowls of more bugs than I'd ever imagined eating. They even had a television crew on hand to film the event. Hornet vodka and spider liqueur began making the rounds, as folks laid their buggy bounty on the low tables. There were bowls full of tiny mantises; big, brilliantly colored orb weaver spiders; giant mealworms; frozen juvenile Madagascar hissing cockroaches; small brown cicadas*; scary-looking black *zazamushi,* a.k.a. river larvae (*zaza* is the onomatopoeic sound of a river rushing, and *mushi* means "insect"—it refers to any of the nymphs found in moving water). One of my favorite dishes was the sugared black sakura caterpillars, which feed on the famed Japanese cherry blossom trees. They were as sweet and tasty as their preferred diet, accompanied by the pink, flowery imagery they evoke.

Most of the insects were fried in vegetable oil. Groups then sat and punched out *nigiri* (literally, squeezed rice) with plastic molds and placed the fried bugs on top. My first job was at a sushi restaurant, and having seen photographs on the web of Uchiyamasan's famous *mushi-nigiri* (bug sushi), I was extremely eager to try them. The plate of molded rice balls topped with the different shapes and colors of fried bugs was impressive, to say the least.

The fried cockroaches were the best of their kind I've ever tried—Uchiyamasan was right! I was a convert. I don't know how they did it (Japanese culinary magic, I suppose), but the normally tough roaches were light and crispy. Delectable with a spot of wasabi and rice.

The big fried orbs of weaver spiders were something else entirely—my mouth stung slightly as I chewed them, leaving

---

* I remember summers in Japan when the air was filled with the grating wails of those cicadas—a penetrating, looping, buzzing riff; the humid heat made audible. I once heard someone remark that they thought the sound was some sort of machine until they learned it came from insects.

a numbness behind like a stiff shot. They also tasted, for lack of a better word, "buggy," perhaps because their diet—unlike that of the mostly vegetarian roaches—is, well, bugs. The intensification of all those flies and whatnot was less than pleasing.

Then Uchiyamasan brought in a huge hornet's nest.

Japan is home to the largest and most deadly species of hornets in the world. In Japanese they are known as *Oo-Suzumebachi* ("giant sparrow bee"). Each hornet can easily reach well over an inch long and has a quarter-inch stinger with venom so potent it can dissolve human flesh. Every year in Japan, dozens of people die from the stings, making the hornets the most lethal animal in Japan, outstripping fugu, snakes, and bears.

Oo-Suzumebachi are known for their speed and endurance. They can fly up to twenty-five miles an hour and up to sixty miles in a day while foraging food for their young. The adults hunt and then chew up smaller insects to feed as "meatballs" to their larvae; however, the adults have such narrow entrances to their stomachs that they are physically unable to eat this meat themselves. Dr. Takashi Abe observed this and wondered how they were able to have such stamina and energy without food.

He discovered that the larvae, once fed a meatball, secreted a liquid that the adults drank. Dr. Abe analyzed the liquid and found it to be high in seventeen of the twenty known amino acids, several extra beyond what we think of as the essentials. He theorized that this somehow enabled the adult hornets to metabolize the stored fat in their abdomens as fuel. He named the liquid vespa amino acid mixture and synthesized the hornet juice into a product called Vaam. Japanese Olympic gold

medalist and record-breaking marathon runner Naoko Taka-
hashi credits the drink for her winning edge.*

Whether or not the hype is true, I am still excited to eat a
hornet larva.

Uchiyamasan fishes one big white grub out of the nest
with a pair of chopsticks.

"Haribo mitai!" remarks the male TV show host. *It looks
like a gummy worm!*

It does. I eagerly reach for the larva and pop it into my
mouth, to the shock of the TV hosts. It's creamy and tastes
fresh, like a custardy sashimi. *"Oishii desu,"* I say. *It's delicious.*

"Oishii?!" the TV hosts exclaim, incredulous. They've
probably seen Westerners do all sorts of strange things, but
perhaps never relish a raw hornet larva.

As the party gets warmed up, I head off to the restroom,
which has special slippers just for walking around inside.
When I come out, another old friend from childhood has arrived, Rika Hayashi, who is now a documentary filmmaker
in China. She's here to help translate the second portion of
my evening—and thank goodness, because there is so much I
want to know. I'm thrilled to see her, and we hug and squeal.

"So what's the deal with this party?" I ask. "It was such a
big secret."

Rika questions the nearest person. "Oh," she says. "It's a
welcome party for you. You're a star or something." She elbows me in the ribs, winking.

---

* She's not the first record-breaking runner to thank insect-based elixirs for her
success. In the early '90s, Chinese runners drank a tea made from caterpillar fungus. "Perhaps American athletes, faced with the challenge of serious competition
at home during the Atlanta Olympic Games in 1996, will consider altering their
diets," commented *New York Times* columnist William C. Rhoden at the time.
"They may find that it's better to eat worms than dust."

At that moment, I realize I'm still wearing the bathroom slippers—that I have, in fact, worn them around the party for the last several minutes. I might as well have had a toilet seat cover tucked into my skirt. I turn bright red and sprint back to the bathroom, while Rika nearly dies laughing.

"You know, I remember you eating bugs on the playground at school," she tells me when I return. "I think even back then you said they were 'just protein.'"

I am floored. I don't remember this at all. And here I thought I'd kept my eccentricity pretty much under wraps in junior high. Rika shakes her head.

"No one is surprised you've gotten into this," she tells me dryly.

Once a bug-eater, always a bug-eater.

8

When in Thailand

EVERYONE KNOWS THE laws of physics don't apply when driving in other countries. At least, that's what I tell myself as I'm clutching onto the back of a motorbike, squeezing through Friday night traffic in Chiang Mai, Thailand.

"I'm sort of worried about moving back to the US," my friend Ben Pratt shouts above the rumbling din. "I'm afraid I'll get too many traffic tickets. Because here I can do anything I want. Anything. The traffic laws here are really just suggestions."

Ben's ex-girlfriend, Rena Chen, started the Environmental Discourses on the Ingestion of Bugs League (EDIBL) at Princeton. When he first met her, he said, "I did what everyone else does: say, 'That's freaking weird.'"

Then, one night while studying, Rena fell asleep on his couch, her computer open to an article on entomophagy. Ben started reading. Hours later, when she woke up, Ben was still reading article after article about edible insects.

"I thought, 'This is the most interesting thing I've ever heard in my life.'"

After that, his passion for entomophagy snowballed. He decided to start an EDIBL club at his own college. When the student council fought it, Ben fought harder and finally won. He hosted a big edible insects event, and it was covered by *Bloomberg Businessweek*. Now, EDIBL exists in several countries around the world.

For Rena's senior paper on entomophagy, the pair traveled around Thailand doing research. Ben fell in love with the country and moved here a year later when he graduated.

Tonight Ben and I are headed to the Night Walking Market to see bugs sold in stalls. It's called the Night Walking Market because that's what you do: join a dense, murmuring throng of people, and float along like stopped-step flotsam at the pace of the crowd.

I hang on to the strap of Ben's shoulder bag.

Ben's neighbor, Stu, joins us. Stu has a Thai girlfriend, Dia, whose family has offered Stu insects at their home on more than one occasion. The first time, he says, he wasn't feeling well, so he declined.

"'What's the matter?'" he imitates Dia's mother as saying. "'Why won't you eat them? What, do you only eat bread?'"

The second time, Dia's sprightly old grandfather bit off the head of a giant fried grasshopper and offered Stu the rest.

"You don't turn down Grandpa," Stu says. He didn't particularly care for it one way or another. "It was just crunchy," he explains, and shrugs.

We're looking for two things at the market: a fried insect stall and red weaver ant egg omelets. Weaver ants are only in season during the dry months. (Thailand has two seasons, wet and dry.) This is both the dry season for weaver ants and the high season for tourism.

Weaver ants build their nests in mango trees, where they are safer from predators and from intermittent rains that might drown ground nests. They build their nests out of mango leaves painstakingly folded and bonded together through a frankly incredible process of connecting their bodies together until the leaf curls to their collective will, becoming one of the curved walls of their new home. They hang on to each other's petioles, or waists, in long strings. Meanwhile, other workers massage the larvae to release silk, which is used to fasten the leaves together.

Weaver ants are highly aggressive, delivering painful bites to anyone they deem to be a threat to their nests. For this reason, they have been employed by Southeast Asian farmers as natural biocontrol agents since 400 AD — and are given a wide berth.

Farmers help and attract the ants by supplying rope bridges between fruit trees that serve as superhighways that connect colonies and help protect the ants from ground predators and other obstacles. Farmers also often provide food and water for the ants. Fruit trees guarded by weaver ants tend to sustain significantly less leaf damage and to produce higher-quality fruit than those without.

The ants do exact their own payment, however, in the form of aphids. They establish colonies of aphids, tiny, sap-sucking bugs, on various plants in order to "milk" them of their sugary secretions. Basically, there's a farm within a farm. The farmers employ the ants by stringing rope between mango trees. The ants, in turn, farm aphids on the farmers' plants and attack any creatures that threaten their "livestock" or offspring.

During the dry spell in a country that thrives on wet-weather crops like rice, ant eggs provide welcome nutrients such as protein and glucosamine. Unlike most other ant species, which utilize irritating and spicy formic acid as a defense, weaver ants use acetic acid, like the stuff in vinegar, making them more palatable to everyone from humans to apes.

When it's time to collect the return on their investment, the human farmers use long, pointed bamboo poles with bags tied on to them to harvest the ant eggs. They poke a hole into the bottom of the mango leaf nest and jar it until the contents of the nest fall into the bag: eggs, pupae, and adults— the whole shebang. Then they back off for a while to avoid being bitten by the naturally furious worker ants. After the initial fury dies down, and the ants' numbers have dissipated, the farmers return to pour the contents of the bag into a shallow pan and, again, back off to let the adults scatter and blow off steam. What remains is a pan full of the white bean-like eggs and pupae (partially developed ants), and a few diehard adults that won't leave their babies for anything. These are then packaged and sold, live and as-is in the market.

We feel a bit like ants ourselves as we move along with the horde at the market, occasionally breaking off to explore side streets, veins off the main artery, in our hunt for food. We stumble into what looks like a temple courtyard, and there we find the omelet man.

He's got an open grill on which rows of small green banana-leaf boxes sit. He ladles beaten eggs into each of them and then adds a topping of your choice: ant eggs or bee larvae. Basically, the dish looks like a green box with a yellow center and little white globules on top that sink into the egg mixture. While we wait for them to cook, we chat.

Ben waves to one of his students, who seem to be everywhere we go. "I'm not supposed to *wai* them back, since I'm their teacher," he says, referring to the prayer-handed bow used in Thailand to show respect. "It's really awkward." He grunts, making frustrated *wai*-like gestures.

The omelets, delivered with a flourish, are like little leaf boats filled with egg on egg. They are smoky from the grill. The ant eggs lend a slightly sour, slightly liver-y taste, as well as a beady texture. They crunch in your mouth like tiny, meaty grapes. It's not bad—it's neither the best nor the worst omelet I've ever had.

"The fun is the crunch," says Stu.

Later we come upon one of the things I've flown so far to see: a fried insect stall—rather commonplace here in Chiang Mai and in many parts of Thailand. Here, in all their glory, are several fried varieties: three species of crickets—giant, meaty brown ones; smaller black ones; and brown mole crickets with their characteristic handlike forelegs—grasshoppers, silkworm pupae, giant water bugs (listed as "horseshoe crab"), whirligig beetles, tiny cicadas, and bamboo worms. I stand in awe for a few moments. This moment is important to me because the majority of my entomophagy research has taken place in the United States, where eating insects is never normal, never public. And I'm usually the one proffering the fried bugs. To see them, after all these years, as part of a normal cultural scene is sort of like seeing a unicorn. Up until then, it had mostly been a myth I believed in; a distant, hazy memory. Now, it was real.

Naturally, I buy a bag with a few of each species. After a couple of crunchy, somewhat greasy bites, we decide what they'd really go well with is beer. So we hop back on the bikes to find a bar. We find a place almost as stylistically retro as Yoru-No-Hirune in Japan, strewn with art deco furniture, guitars, and an awesome collection of vintage hi-fis and neon diner clocks. We grab our Lion beers and find a spot at a table to eat bugs and shoot the shit.

These bugs, I must say, are probably my least favorite of those I'd eaten on all of my travels, though probably the most commonly experienced by both the locals and visiting tourists. They're all right—about as exciting as corn nuts or sunflower seeds. Locals line up nonchalantly for a bag they can eat while browsing the market stalls, while tourists gawk and freak out and pose for pictures. The bugs have all likely been fried in the same oil, so all have a similar taste, and having sat out for a while they are no longer as crisp and fresh as they could have been. The same, of course, goes for pizza, burgers, and fried chicken. Hot and freshly prepared is no comparison to cold leftovers.

The tiny cicadas are our favorites by far, and we are soon strip-mining the bags for them, like you would for the chocolate chips in trail mix. The Lion beer is good and cold, the slide guitar twangy, and the conversation lively. We stagger home that night, leaving a pile of legs and shells in our wake.

The next day I catch a *tuk-tuk* to Makro, Thailand's version of Costco. After wandering around and marveling at the unexpected foods I find there—whole, gutted frogs on ice in the seafood section, as well as manta rays and sea snails—I end up in the frozen meats section. It's kind of like the menu at the Star Wars Cantina. There's virtually every kind of meat you could imagine and several you would never even suppose existed. Pork lungs, frozen blood, several species of heart, various cuts of crocodile, ostrich, and deer. Then there are the bugs. Nestled between the ostrich patties and the crocodile fillets is a small but solid section of frozen insects in one-kilogram bags. Fat white sago palm grubs stacked together like wontons, frosty crickets, potato string–like bamboo worms, and nutlike silkworm pupae. Just sitting there, like it's normal.

I stand there and stare for a while. Some people fly thousands of miles to see the Taj Mahal, Chichén Itzá, or the Sistine Chapel. I, apparently, had flown this far to stand gaping at the frozen food aisle at Thai Costco.

I feel sort of silly, but I don't really want to leave. All this time back in the States, I'd been thinking and writing and talking and envisioning just this: preserved insects sold in normal food stores for the general public. And here it is, before my very eyes. Tangible at last. If I had a membership (and a kitchen), I could buy a kilo of each of them, bring them home, cook them up, and have a party. This could be Thursday night's dinner. I could make a sago grub casserole or a cricket stir-fry. I could toast up a bunch of bamboo worms for my kids' after-school snack or make a snack mix with the silkworms for my husband's Super Bowl party.

The fact that insects are plentiful and currently available like this in Thailand is a fairly new thing in and of itself. The surrounding countries of Laos, Vietnam, Cambodia, Malaysia, and China all traditionally eat insects to varying degrees. Thailand is, through the help of a few passionate, driven individuals, gradually changing the face of its insect consumption to meet modern needs, even in the face of modernization and Westernization.

Next stop, Phuket. I'm probably one of the only people in the world to travel to this fabulous vacation destination for the bugs, but it's one of the best places to find sago grubs, the larvae of the sago palm weevil. The fried grubs are known as Sago Delight and are considered a special, high-nutrient delicacy. They are supposed to taste like bacon.

My contact, Chalit, was a real estate prospector here in Phuket for many years, then quit to run a clothing store. Now semiretired, he has started a sago grub farm on a friend's rubber tree plantation. It began as a hobby, but he soon realized he could make money off it. On the drive over, he tells me about his plans to turn the farm into a tourist attraction. We spout off potential names: Chalit's Worm Emporium. Sago World. Grubs "R" Us.

Despite his desire to capitalize on the tourist industry in Phuket, he is frustrated by tourism and how it has taken over what was once a sleepy, tranquil, abundantly natural and beautiful area. People sell off their land to developers for big money, he says, but then that's all there is—development. People lose their culture, their pride, their way of life. Everything becomes about tourism. The locals can no longer afford to live in the areas once central to their traditions. Being near the beaches is out of the question. Fishing is harder.

As we drive deeper into the countryside, away from the beaches and citified areas, I can see why people would sell out. Dingy, fragile-looking shacks; open-fronted concrete homes; old people lying on platforms—there don't appear to be a lot of dispensable resources here. While they are clearly rich in natural resources—each plot is relatively large and almost overwhelmingly verdant—it's easy to see how cash in hand could trump fresh pineapples from the garden.

Chalit's friend's plantation looks much the same as many others, minus the pineapple sharecropping. Scrappy, scraggly chickens wander about, eating the abundant wild insects that every step in the tall grass kicks up. And then I see it: my first real edible insect farm.

The farm is mostly just an open shack—like the houses, but minus walls and lined with long shelves, like narrow wooden-planked bunks. Edged up along the shelves are round black plastic bins, like big planters, topped with wooden lids. Chalit lifts one up for me. There, wriggling away from the light like all larvae I've seen, only on a much larger scale, are the sago grubs. They look as though someone has taken a photograph of the tiny wax worms I'd started with and enlarged it about twenty times.

Now, I've been interested in sago grubs for years but have only seen them in pictures. It's long been a goal of mine to taste them.

Chalit and his friend chuckle as I ooh and aah over the baby beetles, occasionally reaching out to tentatively pick one up before it squiggles away. I've been bitten before by big caterpillars, and these guys looked like they had some mandibles on them. I reach out intrepidly and then girlishly squeal away. They are big suckers, the size of my thumb on a fat day, but semitranslucent with a creamy white center. Very much like creased, moving dim sum with a shiny black button for a head.

I bring my nose down to the squirming bin of pumpkin-pie-colored sago palm pulp and its munching inhabitants. It smells faintly of earth and palm wine, but otherwise nothing. I turn my head to lower my ear down to the writhing mass. It sounds like a crackling bowl of Rice Krispies or maybe a tiny auditorium of people slurping noodles. A mushy clicking and smacking. Every so often, I hear a little squeak. Chalit says it's just the bugs' bodies against the wet wood pulp, but I think it's their little caterpillar voices.

Chalit shows me the larger, flatter bin he calls the "honeymoon suite," which houses male and female palm weevils. Decoratively marked and somewhat Halloween-y in orange and black, the weevils are far smaller than the larvae, perhaps a third the size of their chubby, Jabba the Hutt–like offspring. With longish snouts, I think the weevils themselves look a bit like Greedo, the blue dude who confronts Han Solo at the Cantina.

Sago palms tend to grow more abundantly in the south of Thailand, which is why there are more farms here than in the north, where the grubs, ironically, are traditionally consumed. While relatively abundant, sago has a long growing period, and several grub farmers have run into limitations when it comes to sourcing them effectively and reliably. Chalit says he's found an abundant, reliable, alternative source of food that he calls a "garbage plant." He keeps the species of the plant secret because he wants to keep his discovery from the hands of would-be competitors.

Once you feed them, he says, you just leave them alone for about a month to grow to harvest size. He says he checks on them about once a week. Every month, he's producing around twenty-five pounds of the grubs on his tiny hobby farm — not enough, he says, to keep up with demand.

"I have a lady in Udon Thani who wants one hundred pounds a week. I told her to take it easy."

We discuss plans for his tourist project until we can't stand the mosquitoes anymore. Chalit insists on sending me home with a bag of sago worms. Although I'm dying to taste them, I don't have a kitchen. What would I do with a live palm grub? Chalit tells me not to worry, that my hotel's kitchen staff will cook them up for me. His friend agrees and begins filling, and I mean filling, a plastic grocery bag with white worms.

In her book *Animal, Vegetable, Miracle,* Barbara King-solver writes of a similar situation with a Zucche de Chioggia squash that instantly comes to mind. She'd found the big green squash at a local farm stand and been fascinated by it.

The farmer told her to buy one and take it to the kitchen at her hotel, where they could extract the seeds (so she could plant one at home) and cook it for her.

"I frankly could not imagine sallying into the kitchen of our hotel and asking anyone to carve up a pumpkin . . . ," she says.

Imagine doing that with a bag full of giant, wriggling larvae.

It's dark by the time Chalit drops me off, and he's in a hurry to get to his next appointment. We quickly divvy up the grubs, and he pulls away. I cross the street back to my hotel, holding the bag. The doorman, Chakan, waves to me, welcoming me back. Before I chicken out, I hold out the bag of grubs.

Chakan's reaction is priceless—he knows what they are, he recognizes them, but I can guarantee you it's the first time a *farang* (foreigner) has presented him with live grubs to cook. He starts laughing, which catches the interest of the desk clerk, who comes over to see what he's looking at.

Now I'm drawing a bit of a crowd as the rest of the hotel staff comes to see what the fuss is about. Their reactions are a mix of knowing and skeptical smiles, nervous laughter, and outright astonishment—more at me than the contents of the bag. They look in the bag, they look at me, back at the bag. Finally, Pot, the sixteen-year-old waiter, agrees to fry up the grubs, so we all follow him into the kitchen.

Pot turns on the fryer and lets it warm up. Meanwhile, he dumps the grubs into a metal cooking bowl and fills it with water to rinse them off, nonchalantly moving them around with his hand like you might a bunch of fingerling potatoes. Then he quickly pats them dry with a paper towel. They squirm around, not happy about the light and the lack of sago pulp to eat—after all, they've been food-free for about forty-five minutes now. Most grubs I've known are absolutely voracious.

Before I realize what's happening, Pot dumps the bowl of grubs straight into the fryer oil, where the French fries, chicken nuggets, and egg rolls are made. I gape at the bugs, while the others watch me, smiling. Within a few seconds, the grubs have all straightened out, the transparencies at their edges intensifying—they look more like dim sum or wontons than ever before.

Pot lifts the basket, lets the oil drip away, and then dumps the fried sago grubs carefully onto a plate. I stare at them, not quite sure I have the guts. Obviously, I don't have much of a choice now, do I? I order a beer, grab a napkin, and find myself a seat in the dining room.

Everyone follows me, amused, taking seats at the surrounding tables, not wanting to miss my first bite. They set down my beer, and I take a first big sip with a flourish, winking. "Well, here goes," I say, shrugging, and tuck into the grubs with my fingers.

They are squishy to the touch, like big greasy prunes. I bite into one. Instantly my skeptical countenance clears—it's good! It's quite like a potato chip, with a squishy, fatty center. "*A roi!*" I say to my audience. *It's good!* They laugh.

Chakan agrees to eat one. He makes the same face of pleasant surprise. "*A roi, a roi!*" He nods emphatically to the others. *It really is good. The* farang *wasn't kidding.* I don't get any other takers, though. These grubs are more popular as a food item in northern Thailand.

The sago grubs are so rich that I can eat only about five of them before my stomach shuts down. I'm full. I was planning to have them as an appetizer, but I literally have no more room for dinner. Just to be on the safe side, since I tend to get hungry at night, I had ordered a salad, but manage only a few bites of it.

I go to bed mildly queasy, but it's the sort of nausea you'd get after a dinner of fried chicken or some other greasy thing. The next morning, I leave at 5 A.M. for Bangkok, again, en route to my next stop. The staff at the hotel all know me or have heard of me by now, so I receive a warm, chuckling farewell.

I'm headed to northeastern Thailand, near the Laotian border, to a town called Khon Kaen. Khon Kaen has an agricultural university, where entomology professor Yupa Hanboonsong has been studying and teaching about edible insects for over a decade.

Yupa has been teaching farmers in both Thailand and neighboring Laos how to raise crickets for food for nearly fifteen years. In that time, the industry has grown to twenty-five thousand farmers strong. Yupa estimates that between $2,000 and $5,000 can be made every month or so on a good cricket-farming business for an initial investment of maybe $50.

Today, a group of Laotian cricket farmers have come to see how the Thais do it — to exchange both information and genetic material. It's best to have as broad a genetic pool as possible to breed from, so the Laotians will buy and bring back bags of cricket eggs from the Thais, and vice versa.

Our van pulls up in front of a large pink stucco house, the House That Crickets Built. The owner, a cricket farmer, greets us.

"He's an interesting case," says Yupa. "Everything he has now — house, cars, everything — was bought with cricket money."

The farmer shows us around his backyard cricket farm. There is a big wooden beam structure with canvas walls, which can be lifted or tied down depending on the weather. Rows of cement tubs run the length of the "cricket house"; each row is at a different stage of life: tiny pinheads, tender juveniles, adults, and mating chambers. You would think the noise of the chirping would be deafening, but it isn't; it's pleasant. It doesn't smell, either, except for the faint scent of chicken feed. It's all quite tidy, in fact, for livestock. I imagine what this space would be like full of chickens, and there's no comparison. As soon as we get about fifty feet away, you can barely even hear the chirping at all.

The farmer gives a short talk in front of his house, which is noticeably nicer than those of his neighbors'. Their weathered teak shacks don't compare to his Hollywood-esque pink structure, his ornate front gate, his colorful garden of sprawling succulents, fruit trees, and gerbera daisies. The Laotians seem suitably impressed as they stand under his star fruit tree, listening to his rags-to-riches tale. It's a Thai country song played backward: He gets his wife, house, and car back, all thanks to the crickets. He plans to erect a giant cricket statue by his front gate.

"Originally, he was a cattle farmer," Yupa translates for me, "but ran into problems. Cattle are very expensive. They got sick and died. He became bankrupt. His wife threatened to leave him. Then he invested twenty thousand baht [around $700] in a cricket farm. The first month he made back half his investment."

The group laughs. Yupa smiles. "He says he's very grateful for the crickets."

In many ways it's easier to raise crickets in Thailand than

in many other places. The year-round warm weather means no extra energy needs to be spent to keep the crickets at prime growing and breeding temperature. However, cricket farms in the United States, whose market is mainly pet supply stores and fishing bait shops, regularly make millions a year. Ghann's Cricket Farm, which Mike Rowe visited on an episode of *Dirty Jobs,* makes up to $10 million a year—and that's with almost no direct human demand to speak of.

In Thailand, as more people get on board the cricket wagon, prices are becoming more competitive. But they are still good enough that the profits available for such a low investment are pretty hard to ignore.

"Just because this knowledge was forgotten doesn't mean it's not worth knowing," says Yupa.

That evening I go out to dinner with Yupa and a couple of her students. Since ant eggs are in season, we order a variety of dishes with them. My favorite is the ant egg salad, which is like a lighter, pop-in-your-mouth version of ceviche. It is hands-down scrumptious.

The next morning I fly to Phnom Penh, Cambodia. I manage to tear myself away from the manic, vine-wound streets long enough to find a translator for my main purpose here: finding and eating fried tarantulas. It's my last day in Asia, and I plan to spend it stuffing my face with arachnids.

My translator, Levan, and I drive through beautiful, green-quilted countryside. I try to keep up my side of the conversation, but my eyes are locked out the window on rice paddies banked with lotus ponds and dotted with palm trees, thatched-roof houses, and white, floppy-eared Brahman bulls. The scenery is hard to believe. After close to an hour, we pull into what looks like a roadside attraction. A big sign reading SUGAR PALM WORLD stands next to a huge palm fruit flanked by two giant cement tarantulas. This is definitely the place.

First we make friends with the young woman selling tarantulas, Arie, and her two young charges, Srilei and Sreiling, cousins aged eleven and thirteen. I begin patting my pockets, looking for my notebook. In my haste to find it, I bust the zipper off the main compartment of my backpack. Everyone laughs at my hapless slapstick. No longer intimidated, the girls come closer, snacking on fried crickets as we sit and talk.

The red fried tarantulas, called *a-ping* in Khmer, are piled high on a big platter. Srilei's grandmother uses the tarantulas to make a medicinal wine, a wine that "heals a hundred ailments." She uses only the most perfect specimens to make the wine; the rest are eaten, fried in soy oil and seasoned with sugar, salt, and some kind of red seed, perhaps annatto.

Arie says she kills the tarantulas with her bare hands, quickly crushing the carapace with her thumbs before frying them. Here in Cambodia, they eat the tarantulas whole, including their abdomens. They tell me the spiders' bellies are full of herbs, but since tarantulas are predators, I find this unlikely.

After letting a couple of live tarantulas climb around on my shirt, I'm ready to eat what I've come so far for.

We are invited to eat lunch with the owner of this little roadside attraction, Sok Keang, in his restaurant. We thank the girls, who won't leave their post, and bring a couple of the tarantulas inside as an appetizer.

They are quite tasty, like extra-chewy Korean barbecue crossed with a Dorito. I eat my tarantula but stop at one, realizing I oughtn't challenge my stomach too much right before a twenty-hour international journey.

As we eat a wonderful, hearty local soup called *kokor* with a side dish of morning glory greens with garlic and chili, Sok tells us why he started this establishment. There used to be forests, he tells us, full of palm fruits and tarantulas, and people would eat them. These forests are swiftly vanishing, and so are this particular species of palm and the tarantulas. He wants people to remember them, to be inspired to save them. He serves us a dish of the palm fruit that is thick, gummy, and mildly sweet. I find it harder to eat than the tarantula, actually.

We wave good-bye to our friends and speed off back to Phnom Penh as a gauzy dusk falls, tinting the formerly green landscape first pink, then purple, like a bruise. Finally, darkness falls like a plank on the villages as they sweep by out the car window. There's a power outage, and people are gathering in houses and shops with lanterns and candles, giving it all a rustic, intimate feel. I know history has not been kind to this place, and that while other countries move steadily forward, the people here have had to rebuild again and again from the ground up.

It's easy to think that people in less developed parts of Asia eat insects only because they have to. Some historians have suggested that the native Cambodians only began eating tarantulas out of pure hunger during the rule of the Khmer Rouge, when food was hard to come by, though other sources show that these animals were considered edible long before that.

While it's true that hunger is the great equalizer when it comes to defining edibility, Asia has such a deep and abiding history of eating insects that dismissing the whole thing as desperation is a big, and ultimately unhelpful oversimplification. There are plenty of places where certain insects cost more than other types of meat on the market, places where they are considered a special treat, a delicacy. Perhaps, yes, a throwback to earlier times, but comfort food is comfort food. We relish plenty of comfort foods in the West that might be considered very strange elsewhere: tuna casserole, made traditionally with smelly, canned fish, mixed with, of all things, fermented cow's milk and canned cream-of-fungus; Jell-O salad, with a main ingredient derived from bovine hooves; Spotted Dick, which in addition to its funny name is made with suet, a raw mutton fat; and haggis, or chopped-up sheep's organs wrapped in its stomach.

Don't tell me people only eat insects out of desperation.

9

The Final Frontier

I N   T H E   E A R L Y   '80s, when entomologist Marcel Dicke
proposed that plants can communicate with the enemies
of their enemies—that they send out chemical beacons
to the bugs that eat the bugs that feed on the plants—his colleagues laughed.

"Plants don't talk," they said. It's a nice fantasy, but it's not
real science.*

But Dicke's doctoral research, performed at the University of Wageningen in the Netherlands, found evidence that
when spider mites attack lima bean plants, the plants release
a chemical SOS that attracts another mite that preys on the
spider mite. It might not be the kind of talking humans do,
but it is communication. It's interspecies communication to
boot.

---

* Granted, this was in the wake of a pseudoscientific book on the subject of plant
communication, *The Secret Life of Plants* by Peter Tompkins and Christopher
Bird, which had been much discussed in the scientific community.

Now, the idea that plant communication plays a role in the biocontrol of pests has been adopted in greenhouses and farms all over the Netherlands.

Despite this, in 1997, when Dicke and a colleague, entomologist Arnold van Huis, began proposing that people should consider eating insects, the chortling began again.

"The responses were, without exception, that we were nuts," says Dicke.

This reaction isn't all bad, admits the man now accustomed to the fringe. At least you have their attention, he says.

"If people think you're crazy, they don't view you as boring. They think you're doing something worth thinking and talking about."

Dicke and van Huis went on a quest to open people's minds to thinking and talking about insects in general, to open the lines of communication between the species, so to speak. Van Huis had spent many years living and conducting entomophagy research in Africa, and brought a great deal of experience and knowledge about native, traditional perspectives on these practices. In addition to their regular teaching and advising load, the two entomology professors began a lecture series called "Insects and Society," which addresses all sides of the human-insect equation. Insects and psychology. Insects and art. Insects and food.

As part of this project, in 2006, they proposed the idea of a City of Insects in their small university town of Wageningen. They would invite people from all over the Netherlands to come and learn about insects, to see them in artistic displays, and even to taste them.

"Fine," said the university event advisory committee. "As long as you realize that no one outside of Wageningen will come to it."

"You'll get maybe two thousand people max," predicted the PR department.

Twenty thousand attendees later, they were forced to eat their words. Reuters covered it. Telephone calls came from China, South America, from all over Europe. Edible insects had been the hook. They'd gotten 1,750 people to eat bugs at once and put Wageningen on the map for entomophagy research.

In 2007, Dicke won the NWO Spinoza Award, the Dutch equivalent of a Nobel Prize. Dicke and van Huis continued their work and in 2009 won a research grant from the Dutch Ministry of Agriculture. They were awarded 1 million euros to study the potential of edible insects as a food source for humans and livestock. When news of the sizable grant got out, Dicke received incredulous calls from his colleagues.

"I thought this was just a hobby!" they said.

In the hands of a few, thoughtful, committed people, even a hobby can change the world.*

At the lab at Wageningen, I get to see some of this edible insect research firsthand. Here in the lab they test for nutritional composition, waste, energy usage, and growth rates to confirm just how sustainable raising insects may be.

PhD student Sarah van Broekhoven grinds up mealworms as a preliminary step to test their nutritional components. She puts about a half cup of preserved mealworms into a porcelain mortar, then pours in liquid nitrogen from an insulated metal canister. The second she finishes pouring she begins grinding

---

* This is a reference to a quote by my favorite anthropologist, Margaret Mead, who said, "Never doubt that a small group of thoughtful, committed citizens can change the world; indeed, it's the only thing that ever has."

the mealworms up with a pestle. A delicate white mist flows over the sides of the mortar, making her look like a witch stirring a tiny white cauldron.

I ask her what the liquid nitrogen does.

"It flash-freezes the mealworms, making them instantly ready for testing."

The next step is to put them in a test tube, add in some hydrochloric acid (HCL, the same acid that's in your stomach), and spin it for a while in the centrifuge. This process breaks down the proteins into their individual amino acids, so they can be analyzed for quantity and quality. It's an accurate way of finding out how much protein is in these bugs and what kind. Van Broekhoven shows me the test tube after it's been separated: There is a slender, clear layer at the top; a wide, cloudy brownish layer in the middle; and a small, darker layer at the bottom.

"The top is fat, the middle is the proteins and minerals and water, and the bottom is fiber," she tells me. It's wild to see the food broken down so visibly into its major components. This is precisely what our stomach, and later the rest of our gastrointestinal system, does during digestion.

Dennis Oonincx, van Broekhoven's colleague, is a PhD student whose research papers on the energetic efficacy and nutritional benefits of raising bugs have been picked up by the international media. They are in many ways the scientific cornerstone upon which the Netherlands bug revolution is based. In 2010, he proved that mealworms, locusts, and crickets would emit fewer GHGs than pigs or cattle when raised on an industrial scale. Two years later he established that this is true for the entire mealworm production process, when compared to beef, pork, or chicken. Maybe more important, it takes a lot less land to produce one hundred grams of protein with mealworms than with pigs, cows, or chickens. The secret is how efficiently they convert their feed to body mass. Less food means less crops, means less land. On top of that, there are no inedible hooves, hides, or bones: The whole animal can be consumed.

Currently, Oonincx is looking into how these insects turn their food into body mass and whether there are ways to produce them even more efficiently. Remember, while other forms of livestock benefit from decades of agricultural research, insect farming has had very little so far. Imagine what things might be like ten, twenty, fifty years from now.

After the lab, I head to lunch with Professors Dicke and van Huis at the appetite-primed Restaurant of the Future, an on-site research cafeteria where in addition to serving food, they record your reactions to the various dishes for purposes of consumer research. Hidden cameras are everywhere, recording your facial expressions as you choose your food and your reaction to new foods (like edible insects), and tracking how long it takes you to pick a salad dressing, how many rolls you take, whether you choose meat or vegetarian options. The software used to read faces was originally designed to observe insect behavior by a former student in Dicke's lab.

Famished as usual in the cold climate, I take too much food and can't finish it. I casually ask them about taking my leftovers with me, knowing I'll probably be hungry again in an hour. The professors blanch.

"We don't really do this here," explains Dicke, while van Huis goes off to at least ask about the possibility of a to-go box.

The idea of taking leftovers from a meal in the Netherlands is frowned upon. The term "doggie bag" is used with a hint of humorous derision. Here in a place so sustainable and energy efficient that the lights go off in the professors' offices unless they wave their hands around periodically, the idea of me taking my leftover food with me is practically preposterous. And it's not just that people are expected to take only what they can eat—I was later taken to a restaurant where *no one* could have finished the enormous, many-coursed portions and still had to walk away from a table piled with remaining delectables because the restaurant had nothing resembling a to-go container. As far as I can parse it, the Dutch don't take leftovers from their meals because to do so is considered cheap behavior, rude even.

Even in a country where sustainable food development is a top priority, it can be difficult to scale cultural walls. Here, the idea of eating insects is not only palatable but worth investing millions of dollars in—yet the idea of taking leftovers from lunch is impossible to swallow. Cultural boundaries can be both immense and resilient, even when they aren't based on logic. In Dutch society, if you ask for a (seemingly logical to an American) doggie bag, "They look at you like you're crazy," confirms van Huis. With barriers like this over leftovers, it's not hard to see why the bias against eating insects has been so hard to reverse.

Van Huis spent several years conducting entomology and cultural research in Africa. When he tried to collect information about who was eating which insects, he ran into barriers. People there, he says, know that even if you do eat insects, "you don't tell that to a white person, because you'll get responses like, 'You're nuts.'"

Several other researchers on indigenous entomophagy have encountered the same problem. Native people who eat insects often won't tell Western researchers that they do for fear of their reaction. Sometimes it's because they themselves have cultural perceptions separating the insects they eat and the insects they don't. Some researchers have found that if they ask the question "Do you eat insects?" the answer will be an indignant no. However, if they ask, "Do you eat [local insect common name]?" they may be more successful.

I experienced this myself once, when I went looking for canned silkworms in Koreatown in Los Angeles. I walked into market after market, asking where the caterpillars were. Time and again, I got frowns and shaking heads. I was practically thrown out just for asking.

"Do you have canned caterpillars?" I asked the store manager at the last market on my list. "Insects?"

"No, no," he said, looking at me funny. "We don't have that. No."

Finally, it dawned on me to ask for them by their Korean name.

"How about *beondegi?*"

His eyes lit up. "Oh, *beondegi!*" he cried, clapping his hands together. "You like *beondegi?* Come, I show you!" He personally led me to an aisle with a whole section of the canned pupae, calling out excitedly in Korean to employees we passed on the way and pointing at me. They all smiled warmly.

Partly it's a cultural distinction—to a Korean, there is as much relationship between the average caterpillar and this traditional, prepared pupae as there is for us between crawfish and lobster, or goldfish and anchovy. We happily eat anchovies and other small fish, but imagine the look you'd give someone who suggested you grill up Goldie.

These distinctions run deep.

An association of Dutch insect farmers, VENIK, started the Flying Food initiative, a project designed to teach insect-farming skills to hungry villages in Kenya. The idea was inspired by Bart Hogebrink's 2010 FoodFactory invention—to turn oil barrels, found in nearly every region of the world, into portable insect farms. The idea was that the bugs could be fed otherwise inedible food scraps and compost to produce protein for hungry villagers. Since a great deal of hunger aid projects are built on the idea that food must be created elsewhere and imported to the hungry areas, the Flying Food initiative promises an alternate route to this consistently problematic traditional model. Politics, corruption, and mistargeting all get in the way of the intended distribution of imported food. Also, flooding the market with free food can harm the livelihood of local farmers. Teaching insect farming might be a way to heal the problem from the inside out. The initiative hopes to teach poor farmers a trade that they can use not only to feed their families but to also increase their own income.

But Marijke de Graaf, a spokesperson for the project, told me they often run into some surprising, unforeseen cultural barriers. The project partners with Bondo University in Kenya, in a region where not only is eating many species of insect accepted, but they are known to fetch a high price on the market. However, their traditional method of procuring insects is wild harvesting. Early fieldworkers had to get the locals past the idea that insects are only foraged from the wild and get them to accept the idea of farming insects.

The second barrier they were surprised to encounter was

species related. In the particular province where they were working, grasshoppers were eaten, but not crickets. It took some convincing to show the local Kenyans that the farmed crickets were just as good a food as the wild grasshoppers.

The point is that even these seemingly minor cultural values, while they may appear trivial or arbitrary from an outsider's perspective, can nonetheless be significant detractors from the inside. The Dutch don't take leftovers. The Kenyans don't raise crickets. Americans don't eat terrestrial arthropods— only aquatic ones.

Up until now, the tide has been going against entomophagy, guided by the moon of popular Western culture.

Dicke told me about a psychologist who'd spoken at their lecture series. This psychologist had married a Thai woman and thus spent a lot of time in Thailand. He'd noticed that when a village got a TV the residents gradually stopped eating insects.

This is one clear example of something scholars have long feared—that the expansion of communication networks carrying mostly Western culture might be stamping out local cultural variations in favor of one overwhelming monoculture. Many cultures, especially developing cultures, emulate the image of the West they see on television, hear in music, and taste in the fast-food chains exported from America and Europe. Western ideals have permeated nearly every nook and cranny of the planet.

If people see more Westerners eating insects, it's possible that we could reverse the tide toward a more sustainable alternative. That's why my motto is "Eat bugs, save the world." In addition to the sustainability of the insects themselves, every time you eat an insect, you support the traditions of those who may be losing theirs.

Van Huis says that the Food and Agriculture Organization is glad that the Netherlands has taken such a strong initiative on the subject and that it doesn't have to come from an African or Asian country.

"If a Western country suggests it, there's less prejudice," he says.

Today, the research at Wageningen University leads the world's scientific entomophagy discussion. In 2013, in conjunction with van Huis's team's findings, the United Nations released a two-hundred-page report, entitled "Edible Insects: Future Prospects for Food and Feed Security." The paper touts the nutritional and environmental benefits of insects both as food for people and livestock, includes a cultural background on entomophagy, lists nutritional content, explores resource usage, and proposes possible ways to increase the consumption and maximize the potential of edible insects in the future.

So far, the report has been downloaded from the web 6 million times.

Epilogue

First they ignore you, then they laugh at
you, then they fight you, then you win.

— MAHATMA GANDHI*

THE WORLD IS still a big enough place to include a
vast spectrum of cultural mores. In some places, the
following will fly: fried tarantulas in market stalls, frozen silkworms in supermarkets, or, apparently, being asked to
cook up a bag of live larvae for a hotel guest. In others, asking
for something as simple as a to-go box is met with barely dis-
guised derision.

The world can sustain this diversity, but we have to diver-
sify our sustenance if our planet is to remain big enough to
feed us all. Our relationship with meat is complicated. The resources we have available are finite, and at some point in the

---

* Gandhi toted around his own goat to make sure he always had goat milk.

near future, we will have to choose between our steaks and ourselves.

Not all meat is bad. However, the consequences of how we currently produce and consume meat are real. Meanwhile, the convictions we hold about insects are almost always false. The truth is, you can pretty much take everything bad you know about meat production, flip it upside down, and you've got edible insects. Yet bugs are the ones most vigorously maligned.

Since I began advocating eating insects, I've learned to expect a few routine reactions, especially online where there is a comments section. Not including the hyperbolic shrieks of horror, there are what we entomophagists like to think of as "the usual suspects." First, there's the person who just writes, frequently in all caps, "NOPE." Then there's the guy who writes, slightly more politely, "No thanks, I'll stick to steak." Thanks, guy, but we've got a world to feed here.

Nine times out of ten the next person to pipe up will be the token vegan or vegetarian, who says something to the effect of "Why even consider eating insects? Why not just stop eating animals altogether?"*

Absolutely a reasonable question. Let's explore it. Indeed, why can't we all be like the vegetarian Brahman-Hindus of India, getting our milk from happy, gentle, revered local cows?

India, the world's largest consumer of dairy products, is also home to the world's largest population of cows, and all those cows are doing their ruminant thing, eating vegetation

---

* Sometimes they will link to a picture of a cow or gorilla, wondering why no one asks where these massive animals get their protein. After reading the section of this book on how meat is made, I hope you will be able to handle this misinformed piece of propaganda on your own. Here's a hint: It's the bacteria, stupid.

and burping up a methane storm. In order to keep up with population growth in the next ten years, India will have to increase dairy production (and its methane byproduct) to nearly double what it is today.

Think for a minute about how India will produce all this dairy. In order to keep a cow in milk, she needs to have calves. Half of those calves are male, and male cows do not give milk (they are also troublesome to keep around, being territorial and prone to either fighting or trying to mate with everything in sight). So, what do these gentle, ghee-loving vegetarians do with all the extra cows that are created? They turn them loose to wander the countryside or city streets where they often end up malnourished, eating garbage, getting hit by cars, or dying of disease. The milking cows fare no better—once they have passed the age of milk production, which only lasts a few years—these revered animals are either sold to a butcher or are gently turned loose so they can wander around until they slowly starve to death.

Thus, dairy-supported vegetarianism, as kindly as it is intended, is ultimately upheld by the meat cycle. Frequently, *someone* is eating the meat by-product of the dairy process, or the animal just wanders around till it dies. Not to mention that no one in the US would agree to cows roaming the streets and holding up traffic. It's not nice to the cows, and the people wouldn't stand for it, just like we don't stand for stray dogs, cats, and horses roaming around.

If vegetarianism isn't the answer, then the only thing left is veganism.

Men from the ages of twenty to forty can frequently make a go of veganism, but children, pregnant women, and the elderly are not generally designed to be sustained by veganism alone. Some of the first strict vegetarians/vegans were monks, who spent much of their time meditating. They certainly weren't having babies—a notably high-nutrient-requiring endeavor—and running households. However, when veganism doesn't work out for people because it has resulted in drastic health problems, they are often accused by the vegan community of "having done veganism wrong."

These conscientious would-be vegans, by and large, are reasonably well-to-do first worlders with access to pretty much anything money can buy, nutritionally speaking. They have health food stores carrying vegan dietary supplements from every corner of the globe at their disposal. They are smart, well-educated, well-read people who understand that veganism isn't just peanut butter and tempeh.

It's *hard* to do vegan right, even with so many foods at your fingertips.

While I think veganism is an admirable philosophy—especially when it's based in true empathy for all living things, not just the non-human ones—it's not a realistic choice for all or even most humans living on Earth. It's certainly not fair to expect someone who struggles to get enough to eat to limit their own biology according to a philosophy that nature itself doesn't seem to echo. So what, only poor people eat meat?

It's also not a reasonable answer for many communities around the world. Forget being vegan and eating locally if you happen to live in a place with, say, seasons. Or the desert. Or Nepal, where adequate arable land and the required resources to grow crops just don't exist.

If vegetarianism doesn't work, and veganism doesn't work, what's left? I believe that insects are a part of the answer to this question. So are polyfarms like Joel Salatin's. So is eating local (when possible), and buying humanely-treated, pasture-raised livestock. That livestock could include insects, if we could only get our minds around it.

Let's return, for a moment, to the restaurant of the future, McImpacts, we visited in chapter one. Imagine that instead of ordering the cow burger or the chicken breast, you order the McMeal Burger. A light but satisfying mixture of chickpeas, ground mealworm flour, pureed vegetables, and spices, it's crisp on the outside, savory and soft on the inside. It's light like a veggie burger, but the animal protein in it satisfies your hunger for hours. The essential fatty acids support your brain, nerves, and skin, and the extra calcium means you can forget to take your supplement today. Or perhaps you order a burger with a Crix™* boost, a cricket-based protein and iron powder that gives the burger extra nutrients and a nutty flavor.

Maybe you're a working mom bringing your kids in for a quick supper after day care. They order the Caternuggets. You don't have to worry about things you ordinarily would, like where the chickens came from—all the insects are organic and locally raised. You yourself order a salad with a Crix-infused dressing. You know you're getting all the nutrients you need without overspending on calories. You feel great, and the kids are happy. It's like fast food used to be—easy, quick, reliable, and actually good for you.

Obviously, the possibilities go beyond fast food. Say you're a guy coming home from a long day at the office. Your wife has prepared a Crix-supplemented pasta. It's a lot easier to eat mostly vegetarian meals now that the carbs are also the protein source. It's such a simple go-to at the supermarket. No more agonizing over how the cow was treated, whether the

---

* Not a real product. Yet.

chickens were free-range, if the fish was wild-caught, and if you can afford it. There are always the ento-protein alternatives, which are delicious and healthy.

The entomophagist's meal of the future may be closer than you think. A London-based start-up called Ento, cofounded by Aran Dasan, has come up with its own insect meal of the future: the Ento Box. Made of bite-sized, multicolored cubes, all of which taste a little different and offer a complete set of nutrients, it's kind of like Lunchables meets Soylent Green— only in this case, Soylent Green is bugs. And that's not bad.

The idea, says Aran, is to present consumers with an option that's tasty and familiar to the person eating it, while also being ethically appealing. "You can go into a shop and order this food, safe in the knowledge that you're getting something really delicious and really sustainable. It's going to be good for you and the environment," says Aran. "At the same time, you feel like you're eating something fun, colorful and shareable, a lot like sushi is."

So far, public reactions to Ento's food have been overwhelmingly positive.

"The only complaint we get is that there's not enough insect. People come expecting a whole bug on their plate, so when they're presented with something beautiful but with no visible bugs, they're disappointed. Maybe we should have them come round the back for the whole bugs," he jokes, laughing.

I've had the same experience when I cater events or do cooking demonstrations. By and large, the scariest, biggest, and most visible bugs go first. If I'm cooking scorpions and crickets, the scorpions are gone long before the crickets are. There seem to be two sectors of the market: those consumers who like to challenge themselves and have an exotic, memorable food experience, and those who are a bit more timid and prefer not to see what they are eating. Which brings me back to Soylent Green, the little pea-colored crackers fortified with an animal protein.

The science-fiction novel on which the movie *Soylent Green* was based, *Make Room! Make Room!* by Harry Harrison, is set in a world where, like ours, the human population has reached 7 billion. Food and water shortages abound, and land space is severely limited. A processed food product made of soybeans and lentils, called "soylent steaks," has become such a precious commodity that a store sale on them creates a riot. If Harrison had considered the potential of edible insects in writing his influential story, perhaps the future might not have looked quite so bleak. The same people rioting for soylent steaks could have been raising perfectly nutritious, tasty animal protein right in their own presumably cramped apartments.

I don't need to refer to dystopian science fiction novels to make the point that humanity has gotten too big for its britches. We are bursting at the seams! We simply can't afford to keep on keeping on the way we have been. There is a limit to what our planet can sustain, and we have reached it. Our resources have reached the end of their collective rope.

On the one hand, we should feel proud. Yes, proud. We've been more successful than nearly any species on Earth, except maybe ants. In many places on the planet, just surviving is so far back in our rearview mirrors that we can't even remember what it was like to have to struggle for existence. Humanity is good at what it does. It adapts.

Our ability to adapt and thrive is not marred by the fact

that we have now surpassed our planet's ability to sustain us. Our overuse of resources is quite natural and not all that unique to us as a species. Most animals will consume all the food that is available to them, and breed to their fullest ability, until lack of resources causes them to die off, and the cycle begins again. We shouldn't necessarily feel bad for having reached this point. However, now that we are standing, lemminglike, at the brink, we can be wise about how we venture forward. We can adapt to our situation, just as we always have. It's our best skill and our best bet for the future. Change has always been our constant.

If we need to change by expanding our diets to include insects, well, luckily, that skill is in our wheelhouse. It always has been. Adapting is what makes us *us* in a more fundamental sense than our cultures alone. We can surpass our cultural viewpoints to survive as a species. First, we are human. After that, we are American, Japanese, Dutch, Zimbabwean, etc. Assuming we can get past our cultural biases (and history shows that we can), we should take full advantage of the bounty of protein, essential fats, and minerals that exists all around us in the form of insects.

If you want to be among the first adapters—the group that leads the rest of humanity into the future—there are plenty of options at your fingertips.

In addition to Ento, there are currently a handful of other companies making edible insects readily available to the public. Chapul is already selling its bars in health food stores around the United States, and they can also be purchased from a few international distributors or on the company's website. Don Bugito has recently released gourmet dried mealworm and cricket snacks, available from select retail sources. Companies like World Ento have been selling organic mealworms and crickets for more than a year. You could have a ready-to-eat, edible insect product on your doorstep by next week if you ordered it today. The fact that these products exist is new, and it's exciting. Nothing quite like this has ever happened before. However, the idea itself isn't new, only re-packaged. Humanity has eaten insects for millennia. Some of us fell out of the habit of it. But, like riding a bike, perhaps it will come back to us with practice. We might feel a bit shaky at first, but over time, it may begin to feel natural again.

I am not going to suggest that this idea is for everyone. Most people on this planet struggle to get enough to eat every day, let alone have the ability to choose from a miraculous, over-whelming bounty of options, and decide what is the right thing to eat for the right reason. High carb, low carb, or no carb? Meat or processed vegetable protein? Gluten-free or lac-tose-free? The China Study or the Paleo Diet? Weston Price or Dr. Weil?

But for those of us who can choose, we owe it to ourselves and to the world to choose wisely. To choose well for those who have no choice. While I'm not sure I believe in trickle-down economies, I do believe in trickle-down social attitudes. I believe the few can lead the many, and that word of mouth works. And I believe that ending the war on bugs might result in a greater quality of life for all involved—even the bugs. A softening of our knee-jerk, "Kill it!" philosophy regarding in-sects, arachnids, and their slimier invertebrate cousins, snails and slugs, could result in greater overall interspecies harmony. Fewer pesticides, more mouths fed, less general shrieking. If there's a downside to including insects in our diets, I don't see it.

The edible insect revolution is happening (and yes, it's being televised). Insects are the great untapped resource, the final frontier of natural food. Lab-grown meat is on the horizon, but with the backlash against genetically modified produce, who's to say how well it will go over in the market or if it can be made cheaply enough to sell to the public. If people don't want to eat DNA-adjusted corn, will they really want to consume great quantities of something created entirely outside the bounds of nature? Will you?

There's a great political cartoon where a guy at a climate summit is saying to his compatriot, "What if it's a big hoax and we create a better world for nothing?"

That's how I think of eating insects. There is so much for it, and almost nothing against it, if we can only get over our prejudices. In a hundred years, it will probably be so common that no one can imagine a world without it. Such a world would seem very backward, indeed.

Acknowledgments

First and foremost, I'd like to thank my husband, Brian, who has supported me through the entire process of writing this book. He helped me invent and test recipes, was a calm and constant sounding board for ideas and frustrations, and was a true partner in all senses of the word. I can't imagine life, or this book, without him.

I'd also like to thank my mother for her creative, yet sharply scientific outlook on life. I wouldn't be who I am without her or my patient, ever-supportive father, who didn't bat an eye when I said I wanted to pursue this subject.

I would of course like to thank all the authors and researchers who came before me, whose work paved the way for this book to exist: Vincent Holt, F. S. Bodenheimer, Ron Taylor and Barbara Carter, Julieta Ramos-Elorduy, Maurizio Paoletti, David George Gordon, Peter Menzel and Faith D'Alusio, and Florence Dunkel and Gene Defoliart. Also, all my friends in the entomophagy field, without whose help, encouragement, and general brilliance, I could never have come this far. David Gracer, Zack Lemann, Brent Karner, Dianne

Guilfoyle, DGG, Harman Johar, Ben Pratt, Rena Chen, Aaron Dossey, Paul Landkamer, Florence Dunkel, Frank Franklin, John Heylin, Mark Finke, Treena Joi, Rosanna Yau and Monica Martinez, Mark Berman, Art Evans, Joanne Lauck, Marcel Dicke, Arnold Van Huis, Marian Peters, and Bart Hogebrink.

Thanks to Marlboro College and anthropologist Carol Hendrickson for leading me down this path to begin with.

I'd also like to thank Carol and Glen Fuerstneau, Nova Bronstein, Paula Sperry, Katie Koralek, David Z. Morris (and his amazing eye for editing), Jace Harker, Lorrie Castellano, Mikiko Baba, Rika Hayashi, Rhys Southan, and David Moye.

Last but in no way least, I'd like to thank my agent, Adriann Ranta, and my editor, Katie Salisbury, for believing in this project.

How to Raise Bugs at Home

Raising insects is relatively easy, requiring about the same amount of time and attention as growing tomatoes. Compared to other forms of livestock, they take very little initial investment and not much space. As you may have noticed if you've ever opened a bag of flour or cereal and seen bugs crawling around inside, it doesn't take much to get bugs breeding. Significant quantities of edible insects can be raised in a space as small as a closet or even a cabinet. The main things they need are plenty of food, a little water, and warmth: 75 to 90 degrees is a good range to keep them eating, growing, molting, and breeding new generations.

The great thing about raising your own insects is that you will always know what the protein you're creating for yourself is made of. You can experiment with different types of feed and see if it alters the insects' flavor. You can also supplement their diet with vitamins and minerals as a way of increasing your own intake.

Traditionally, insects have been foraged, not farmed, which is likely why the idea is still catching on. In places like

Thailand, insect farming is becoming increasingly popular, not only to produce food but also to enhance income. Since insect farming is already a multimillion-dollar industry here in the United States, the future looks bright.

Mealworms

World Ento, founded by Harman Johar, is a company that sells organic mealworm flour and preserved crickets and mealworms. Johar started the company in the closet of his college dorm room and now sells his product in five countries to more than four hundred customers.

"2014 will be the year of the bug," Johar predicts.

Johar's business has far outgrown its original humble digs, and he now uses a much more sophisticated, fully sealed, temperature-controlled setup. For a beginner starting at home, however, he says, "You don't need all of that." After all, he started in a closet.

Johar recommends beginning with mealworms because raising them on a small scale is relatively simple, and even if they do escape, they can't get very far. A cricket, by contrast, might have a leg up when on the lam.

"It's important to understand the organism you're working with," says Johar.

What you'll need to start your mealworm farm (you can, of course, start smaller):

> 40 lbs rolled oats
> 20-gallon plastic bin
> Apples and carrots, chopped
> 1000 mealworms (darkling beetle larvae)
> Heating pad or lamp

1. Grind the oats coarsely in a blender to give the mealworms plenty of surface area to latch onto.
2. Fill the bin about a quarter full with the oats. Distribute the apples and carrots around the surface. You'll be changing the produce out every day or so, so don't chop these too finely.
3. Carefully inspect your mealworms. Put them in the refrigerator for an hour or two to slow down their systems so they

don't crawl all over the place, then spread them out on a tray so you can see them. Remove dead mealworms, which will appear dark in color, as well as pest beetles and their larvae, specifically those of the dermestid beetle.

"If even one of those pests gets in, it can be a real problem," says Harman.

The pest larvae are easy to pick out as they are black with spiky hairs. They are not dangerous, though we don't know if they're all that palatable. The best thing to do is to put these unwanted guests into a container that you then freeze for several days, effectively killing the intruders. Then they can be thrown away.

4. Release the mealworms into the bin. They might be shy at first, planting themselves in the safety of the oats, but they will soon begin devouring their edible home world.

5. Punch a dozen or so small holes in the bin's lid for airflow. Although they aren't likely to be able to climb the sides of the plastic bin, you'll want to keep a lid on Planet Mealworm to keep other bugs from getting in.

6. Every day or so, open up the bin and change out the carrots and apples and remove any dead mealworms or rotting fruit to avoid mold and microbes. Keep the bin's contents as dry as possible — at this stage in the game, moisture buildup can cause more harm than good. Keep the bin warm: 75 to 80 degrees, a temperature that will keep the mealworms eating and molting and breeding quickly, works well for most folks. Heat lamps or pads can be purchased for this purpose.

7. After about a week, check the bin for small black beetles. These are the adult darkling beetles. They will have mated by now and the females laid too-tiny-to-see eggs in the bottom of the bin. These will hatch in two or three weeks. Keep feeding them. Once they are big and plump, you can, if you wish, harvest about half of them for eating.

Johar suggests not harvesting until your second or third generation for one reason: You want to make sure you un-

derstand your livestock before you harvest. Also, he offers a
warning to aspiring mealworm ranchers.

"You may feel an attachment to your first generation," he
says. "When we first saw those baby mealworms coming up,
we felt so proud, like grandparents. But the feelings of love
disappear after the third generation." He laughs.

When you're ready to harvest, place the plump mealworms into a container for freezing. After a day or so, they
are ready to cook. Experiment with their diet to see if you
can subtly alter the flavor of the mealworms.

Crickets

When I toured village cricket farms in rural Thailand, I was astonished at how simple they were. Bathtub-size, uncovered cement vats were the main "plots," and each facility was open to the elements, save for a thatched roof and rolled-up canvas walls. Despite the thousands of chirping crickets, the only smell was that of cornmeal. They were the most pleasant livestock yards imaginable.

The Thais can get away with this setup because of their climate. It's warm there year-round, the perfect temperature and humidity for breeding insects. Certain areas of the United States come close to this as well, which is why there are so many cricket farms in the South.

Although an open-air backyard cricket garden may seem an ideal way to raise crickets, not many of us here in the United States can get away with it, weather-wise. Raising crickets indoors has its advantages. You can more closely control the environment and keep them safer from predators, parasites, and diseases.

What you will need:

> 20-gallon plastic bin
> 10-gallon plastic bin
> Transparent adhesive tape
> 6 or 12 egg cartons or egg flats
> 2 four-inch plastic bowls
> 2–4 cups sand
> Sponge or paper towels
> 2 cups cornmeal
> 1–2 shallow bowls
> Apples and carrots, chopped
> Aluminum mosquito screen
> Duct tape
> 250 crickets
> Heating pad or lamp

1. Line the interior rim of both bins with the tape. The crickets won't be able to climb this slippery surface, thereby reducing escapes.
2. Place egg flats vertically along one side of the 20-gallon bin.
3. Fill one 4-inch bowl with the sand, at least 3 inches deep. This is the nesting material where the crickets will lay their eggs. Mist it thoroughly so that it is damp. Place bowl in bin.
4. Moisten the sponge or folded paper towel and place it in the second 4-inch bowl. This is the water bowl. Crickets will drown in open water, so keep the sponge moist but not dripping. Place bowl in bin.
5. Place cornmeal into shallow bowl, with chopped fruits and vegetables on top. This is the food dish. Make sure it is large enough for many crickets to eat at once, or provide two food dishes. Place bowl(s) in bin.
6. Cover the bin with aluminum screen and secure with duct tape, or create a fitted frame. Don't use plastic for this part as the crickets can chew through it.
7. Check crickets for unwanted guests, then release them into their new home. Change food and water every few days, and make sure the sand, or nesting material, is kept moist. Keep everything else, besides the water dish, dry. Keep the cricket farm warm, about 80 to 90 degrees. Use a heating pad or lamp if necessary.

After about a week, check the nesting material. If it is full of tiny white eggs, transfer it to the smaller bin. Replace it with a fresh container of sand.

The second bin is a miniature of the first bin, so set it up accordingly. Make sure there's plenty of food for the baby crickets once they hatch.

Keep the "nursery" bowl warm and moist while the eggs are incubating. Lightly place a cover on top, enough to keep warmth and moisture in, but also so the baby crickets can get out and hop around the bin once they've hatched. Newborn crickets are so tiny they are called pinheads, but with lots of food and enough warmth, they will begin to grow. Once crickets have reached about 1/4 inch long, they may be returned to the breeding bin. Harvest about half once they are between 3/4 and 1 inch long. Freeze in an airtight container, rinse, and eat.

Wax Worms

Breeding wax worms is like a cross between breeding meal-worms and crickets. Like mealworms, wax worms need a tasty substrate to eat while they are larvae, and like crickets, they also need a specialized place to lay their eggs once they've mated. Wax moths prefer to lay their eggs in nooks and crannies, so you will need to provide these.

> 2 wide-mouthed gallon jars
> Aluminum screen or nylon stocking
> 4 cups oat bran
> 2 cups honey
> 1 cup glycerin
> Waxed paper
> 100 wax worms
> Rubber bands
> Heating pad

1. Boil jars and tops (the screen or stocking) to sterilize.
2. Mix oat bran, honey, and glycerin together. Allow to harden, then break this substrate into chunks.
3. Place crumbled oat mixture into first jar.
4. Crumple balls of waxed paper, making lots of nooks and crannies for the wax moths to lay their eggs. Place these on top of oat mixture.
5. After carefully inspecting wax worms (see mealworm procedure) release them into the jar. Secure mesh over top with rubber band. Keep jar warm (using the heating pad, if necessary) and in a dark place.
6. After 2 to 3 weeks, begin to watch for moth emergence from the pupae in the oat bran. Once the moths begin to die (indicating that they have already mated and laid eggs), transfer the waxed paper balls to the second jar, which should

be set up like the first jar. The eggs will hatch, and the baby wax worms will eat the new substrate.

After about 8 weeks, the wax worms will be ready to harvest. Harvest half, and keep the cycle going. Freeze in an airtight container, rinse, and eat.

The Essential List of Edible Insects
Bugs you can eat, from A to Z!

In general, when trying to ascertain a bug's edibility, there are a few rules to follow—though there are frequently exceptions to those rules.

The main rule of thumb is in the form of a rhyme invented by David George Gordon in *The Eat-a-Bug Cookbook:*

Red, orange or yellow, forgo this small fellow.
Black, green or brown, go ahead and toss him down.

There are two ways to look at this. On the one hand, a brightly colored insect is advertising to the rest of nature that it is not good to eat. Its colors are a neon sign to predators saying, essentially, "I'm not worth it." This phenomenon is called aposematism—*apo* for away and *semantic* for sign or meaning.

Sometimes these insects contain toxic compounds; sometimes they taste bitter, smell bad, or have stinging hairs. Ladybugs are an excellent example. Their shiny red shells may look pretty to us, but to birds they are a warning of intense distastefulness. When threatened, they secrete a bitter-tasting, foul-smelling alkaloid called precoccinelline that pretty much ruins a bird's day.

Meanwhile, black, green, and brown insects are often practicing "safe 'sects" by camouflaging themselves in with their surroundings. Green insects blend in with leaves and grass, brown insects with bark and dirt, black insects with shadows and rocks. They're like buried treasure—they're good to eat and they know it, so their survival strategy is to hide. This phenomenon is called crypsis, and can include camouflage, living underground, being active only at night, and biomimicry.

Naturally, the question many people ask at this point is, why don't more edible insects go the aposematic route, faking the rest of nature out regarding their tastiness? The answer is that some of them do, by mimicking their toxic counterparts. This particular form of false-danger signaling is called Batesian mimicry, which, while not named for fictional baby-faced killer Norman Bates, is nonetheless how I remember the term. These bugs do the opposite of the *Psycho* character: They publicly pretend to be more dangerous than they truly are.

As you can see, nature can be a complicated mother. The mnemonic device above is merely a jumping-off point into the world of edible insects, and not the final word. Several exceptions come to mind immediately. Bees, for instance, are yellow/orange and black, an obvious warning pointing to their stingers. However, drone bees, the males, don't sport stingers, and are perfectly good to eat. Meanwhile, many blister beetles are black, green, or brown, the "good" colors, yet contain cantharidin, an irritant that, while being the basis of folk aphrodisiac Spanish fly, is quite toxic if ingested directly.

In the arachnid group, scorpions and spiders are frequently black or brown yet have obvious edible drawbacks. The black widow spider is black—but the red hourglass on its abdomen signals its toxicity. Brown recluses and sand-colored bark scorpions don't do you the same favor.

One thing that helps render most insects edible is the application of heat. Cooking bugs goes a long way toward ensuring their ultimate edibility.

With that in mind, let's take a look at some of the specifics.

Ant

There are approximately 12,500 classified species of ant. E. O. Wilson estimated that at any given time the biomass of ants roughly equals that of humanity. Though found on nearly every continent on Earth, not all species are palatable. Stinging ants, like fire ants, can be particularly dangerous if eaten raw. I once heard about a guy who went to the emergency room after eating just five live fire ants on a dare.

That ants sting makes sense when you learn that they originally evolved from wasps, and are biologically related to bees as well. Ants are in the family Formicidae, and many species secrete a defense substance called formic acid, which gives them a spicy flavor. David George Gordon likes to use dried ants from China in place of pepper.

The average black or brown ant is edible, especially if cooked. It could be argued that heat could even render stinging ants edible, and though this might be true, I wouldn't risk it.

Even tastier than adult ants are their larvae. Known as *escamoles* in Mexico and *kai mot daeng* in Thailand, these have a variety of flavors. Lightly boiled, then spritzed with a little lime, they taste, I've found, a lot like seviche. Sautéed, they taste more like smoky scrambled chicken eggs.

There are a few particularly popular and interesting species of edible ant. *Hormigas culonas,* or "big-butt ants," are commonly eaten in Latin American countries, such as Colombia and Guatemala. When the large queen ants fly out by the thousands to scope for new digs, they are caught in nets and toasted. They taste a bit like bacony sunflower seeds.

Lemon ants are found in the Amazon jungle and are said to taste like just that: a burst of sour citrus.

Honeypot ants have abdomens swollen with a nectar-like substance, which is used to feed other ants, sort of like a "living larder." An excellent bush food, they are dug up from the ground and eaten raw by Aboriginal peoples in Australia.

Ant larva

Pupa forming into an ant

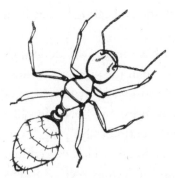

Adult ant

Bee

WARNING: IF YOU ARE ALLERGIC TO BEE STINGS, YOU MAY
HAVE A REACTION TO EATING BEES, EVEN IF THEY'RE
COOKED.

Bee larvae, especially, are prized in many cultures as tasty
morsels. Think about it: All they eat is royal jelly, pollen,
and honey. The larvae, when sautéed in butter, taste much
like mushroomy bacon. Adult bees may also be eaten, often
roasted (roast bee!) and then ground into a nutritious flour.
In China, ground bees are used as a remedy for a sore throat.

In order to get your hands on some of these luscious larvae, ask local beekeepers if they purge their drone combs. The
drones are the male bees, whose main purpose is to mate with
the queen, and they usually exist in excess. Drone bees don't
contribute significantly to pollination, they don't help build
the hive, they don't care for young, and they don't have stingers. They fly from hive to hive, mating and eating honey. It's a
pretty sweet life.

In a beehive, the drones often have their own section, or
comb, because they are a bit larger than the workers, so their
cells have to be bigger. They are also great bait for parasites
(the kind that are only bad news for bees) and freeloaders like
wax moth larvae. Many beekeepers periodically "purge" this
comb by removing it, putting it in a freezer to kill everything,
and then either throwing it away or letting their chickens
peck out the frozen bugs. I say, forget the clucking middle-
men—those larvae are good eating.

If you can talk a beekeeper into giving you the drone
comb, congrats! You'll want to get it into the freezer tout suite.
Once it's frozen, break it into chunks and remove the baby

drones. They'll be in different developmental stages: Some will have almost no features, some will be like little white bees with red eyes, and some will be fully formed. Check for stingers on these, just in case a worker bee got in there.

I suggest keeping the comb fragments as frozen as possible during the extraction process. Don't take the whole thing out of the freezer at once, or the bees will get squishy. I like using a pair of tweezers to gently remove the bees. The extraction process is a lot like seeding a pomegranate — painstaking but worth it.

You can't go wrong with a quick sauté, a little salt, and maybe the tiniest touch of honey. They are simply delectable. Just ask a bear.

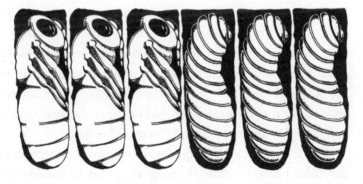

Bee pupae and larvae

Beetle

The word "beetle" is a common term for insects of the order Coleoptera. Coleoptera essentially means "sheathed wing" in Greek, so-called because beetles generally have hard, outer armor—called elytra—that sheath inner, more delicate wings. I think of beetles as having a secret soft self they hide under outer armor.

The Coleoptera are pretty important; 25 percent of all known animals are in this order, and 40 percent of all insects are Coleopterans.

J. B. S. Haldane, one of the founders of the field of population genetics, on being asked what one could conclude as to the nature of the creator from a study of his creation, is known to have replied that the creator must have "an inordinate fondness for stars and beetles."

To put it simply, there are lots and *lots* of beetles. Despite their numerousness, adult beetles are a little less popular as food, as most people and animals tend to prefer them in their larval form. Although many species of adult beetle are in fact edible—and even delightful—they do have those crunchy elytra to deal with. Even birds and bears, enthusiastic insectivores, tend to prefer softer bugs to most beetles.

Scarab beetles are perhaps the most common exception to this rule. There are more than eighty species of edible scarab found in Mexico alone. Dung beetles, worshipped by the ancient Egyptians despite their tendency toward, well, poop, are eaten in certain places in China. Andrew Zimmern ate pot-crisped giraffe beetles in Madagascar and found them to be shrimpy, nutty, and delicious. June beetles are included in the recipe section of this book, and I can vouch for their crunchy, slightly bitter savoriness.

When judging a beetle's edibility, it's best to decide based on its fashion sense and diet. If it's brightly colored and munching oleander, forgo this fellow.

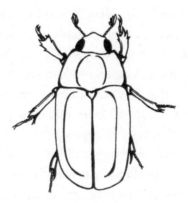

Scarab beetle

Bug

Although we use the word "bug" as an umbrella term to mean anything from an actual insect to a virus, it does have an actual taxonomic meaning. True bugs are insects in the order Heteroptera, and are united by their distinctive arrangement of sucking mouthparts and by having wings that are basically half membranous and half-elytra. When they cross over their backs, you see a nice X shape. Squash bugs, stink bugs, and shield bugs are all true bugs. People in Taxco, Mexico, gather every year to eat and celebrate a certain species of stink bug they call *jumiles,* which they consume live, toasted, or ground into salsa. Andrew Zimmern once said they taste like tutti-frutti, but I think they taste like spicy kale.

Another well-loved true bug is the giant water bug, found in ponds around the world but particularly appreciated by the Thais and Vietnamese. The "essence" of the bug is extracted and sold at market, to be added to sauces and soups. I can attest that these insects have a unique flavor; to me, they taste like banana-infused anchovies soaked in old perfume, which is an impressive sensation to say the least. One tiny bite of their flight muscle will fill your whole head with "essence." Fresh, however, they smell like a green apple Jolly Rancher.

In the United States, these large, predatory insects are known as alligator ticks or toe-biters, for their swift, painful bite.

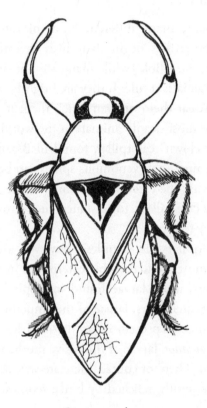

Giant water bug

Caterpillar

There are many, many different kinds of caterpillar. Both moths and butterflies begin their lives as caterpillars, and many of these are edible, while many are not. In general, refer to the aposematism rule: If they are brightly colored, spiky, or hairy, don't eat them or even touch them if you can help it. One of the most deadly animals in the world is the Lonomia, or "lazy clown" caterpillar, found in Brazil. One brush of the skin against their venomous spines can be lethal. Also, be aware of what the caterpillars themselves are eating. Monarch butterfly caterpillars, for instance, ingest toxins from the milkweed they feed on.

Most caterpillars are harmless, however, and very tasty. Some of the most popular edible caterpillars in the world are bamboo borers, moth larvae found in tropical Asian countries; mopane caterpillars, larvae of the emperor moth, are an important source of protein in southern Africa; Agave caterpillars, a.k.a. *gusanos,* larvae of the Agave moth, are considered *rico* in Mexico. Then, of course, there are wax worms, the larvae of the wax moth, relished by birds, reptiles, and humans alike.

White, cream-colored, beige, or light-brown caterpillars are frequently edible. There are several species of bright-green caterpillar that are edible, such as the tomato hornworm (for a great recipe, see Fried Green Tomato Hornworms in *The Eat-a-Bug Cookbook*). *Gusanos* and some instars (life stages) of cornworm are dull red, orange, or pink, proving an exception to the aposematism rule.

Silkworms, caterpillars of the silk moth, are popular in many Asian countries and are eaten in the pupal stage, after they have spun their cocoons of silk. The cocoon is removed, and the pupae are eaten boiled or roasted. Canned silkworm pupae are called *beondaegi* in Korean, and can be found at many Korean markets. I warn you that the canned version is an intense and probably acquired taste (I've been unsuccessful in acquiring it). Don't let it turn you off freshly prepared silk moth pupae, which are delicious, like shrimpy popcorn.

A witchetty grub, by the way, is not a grub but a moth larva found on the roots of witchetty bushes. Eaten by Aborigines in Australia, often roasted in coals or over a fire, witchetty "grubs" are high in protein and fat. According to Peter Menzel in *Man Eating Bugs*, "witchetty grub tastes like nut-flavored scrambled eggs and mild mozzarella, wrapped in a phyllo dough pastry."

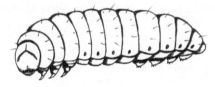

Caterpillar   *Silkworm pupa*

Cicada

Periodical cicadas, primarily found in the eastern United States, live underground for seventeen years before emerging and molting into adults. Just after they molt, they have soft, juicy bodies and are tender and tasty. "They're as soft as crab meat and taste kind of like asparagus," says bug chef Dave Gracer.

Different species of cicada are eaten in many Asian countries, such as Japan, Thailand, and Malaysia.

Forager Paul Landkamer recommends hunting cicadas in areas where they are unlikely to have come into contact with man-made chemicals. Since they sit in the soil for seventeen years, they have plenty of time to absorb all kinds of toxins. Once you've found a suitable area, use your ears to find the best hunting ground, says Gracer.

"Go out at night with a flashlight and look at tree trunks," says Landkamer. After the young nymphs emerge from the ground, they climb up the nearest tree, at whose roots they have spent their life suckling. This is the best time to grab them.

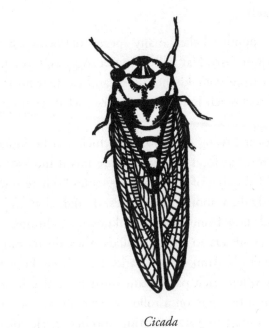

Cicada

Cockroach

Contrary to popular belief, many species of cockroaches are edible and quite tasty. Naturally, I'm not suggesting you pluck a cockroach from your kitchen floor and eat it; who knows where that cockroach has been or, worse, what it's been eating?

Madagascar hissing cockroaches, which can be found in many pet stores as food for reptiles, are raised in clean conditions and fed a diet of fruit and vegetables.* There is nothing inherently dirty about cockroaches, though obviously you should avoid those from urban or unknown conditions.

Known as hissers to their familiars, they do indeed hiss when threatened. Amusement parks have been known to hold events where each participant must eat a live hisser in exchange for a free ride on a roller coaster. There was an insect-eating contest in 2012 featuring another species of large cockroach, the Discoid roach, where a man died. The coroner's report stated that he had choked, probably from not chewing well enough in his haste to get the bugs down his throat.

Obviously, responsible entomophagy enthusiasts don't recommend that you eat any insect live or raw if you can help it. They taste better cooked, anyway, just like many other meats do.

If you are going to eat a cockroach, I recommend eating a juvenile whose exoskeleton hasn't yet become the hard

---

* They also make gentle, interesting pets themselves, actually, and have wonderfully connected societies. I highly recommend them as friends. Having said that, they are also reasonably good eating.

shell of his elders. I had a fried young hisser as a sushi topping in Japan, and it was very tasty, like a tiny tempura-fried
crab.

Some people are allergic to cockroaches, so they shouldn't
partake.

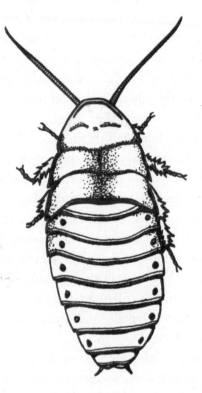

Madagascar hissing cockroach

Cricket

Ah, the ever-charming, highly versatile cricket. Crickets are kind of the chicken of the edible insect world. They are related to grasshoppers and katydids, and generally have a somewhat mild, slightly shrimp-like taste that goes well in lots of dishes. Thanks in part to Jiminy Cricket, they have pretty good PR in Western society, making them seem more friendly and harmless to most people than a larva or a beetle.

They are eaten in Thailand, Cambodia, Laos, and Vietnam, and are usually either fried or pan-roasted. In China and Japan, they are occasionally kept as pets.

A cricket with a long "tail" is a female. This is her ovipositor, which she uses to deposit her eggs safely in the soil. Male crickets are the only ones who chirp, and do so not by rubbing their legs together but by "strumming" one wing with the other. One wing has raised ridges, and the other has a plectrum, which is a fancy word for a guitar pick. When a cricket rubs one wing over the other, the plectrum strums the ridges. Amplified by curves in the structure of the wings, the chirp resonates across the night air: loud for a mating call, soft for courting a nearby female, and occasionally a short burst after a successful tryst.

When you're catching crickets in the wild, a bug net will suffice. Be aware that some species of cricket bite. Wild crickets will be anywhere from black to brown.

I prefer my crickets at about the five-week-old stage, when they are large enough to eat but still tender. I think they go particularly well with garlic.

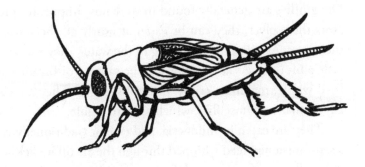

Cricket

Dragonfly

Dragonflies are generally found in wetlands. Impressive predators themselves, they can be eaten at nearly all the stages of their lives. As nymphs, still living in the water, they are said to taste a bit fishy. As adults, they can be sautéed or breaded and fried whole, making a crispy, if fibrous, snack. They are visually similar to damselflies, which are also edible.

They are eaten in Indonesia, and caught traditionally with a sap-moistened reed whipped through the air till it sticks to a dragonfly. I prefer to use a bug net.

It's vital to not overharvest dragonflies. They are important predators of mosquitoes, for one thing, as well as of flies, bees, and other insects.

Dragonfly

Earthworm

Though caterpillars and some grubs are frequently called worms, earthworms are a totally different kind of animal called nematodes. Also known as night crawlers and angle-worms, earthworms filter and aerate dirt, helping to create fertile soil. Charles Darwin said, "It may be doubted whether there are many other animals which have played so important a part in the history of the world, as have these lowly organized creatures."

Because they quite literally eat dirt, it's necessary to purge them thoroughly before eating them yourself.

"Earthworms eat and expel material equal to their weight every twenty-four hours," says the book *Entertaining with Insects*, which suggests that placing them in moist cornmeal or flour for twenty-four hours should effectively clear their systems of soil. After that, they can be boiled for about ten minutes, although some folks prefer to boil them repeatedly, changing the water each time. Once boiled, earthworms can be sautéed, fried, or roasted. Dried and ground, they will make a highly nutritious flour.

In my experience, earthworms taste quite iron-y, which makes sense as they are very high in iron, as well as protein. It may be for this reason that they are eaten by pregnant women in certain South American tribes. They are also considered a delicacy, known as *noke,* by the Maori of New Zealand. *Entertaining with Insects* has several recipes for them.

Sometimes when you pick up an earthworm, which stresses the worm out, it "pees" on you. This secreted liquid is not really urine but instead some of the fluid that gives the worm its shape, keeping it plump. It is, for lack of a better word, worm juice.

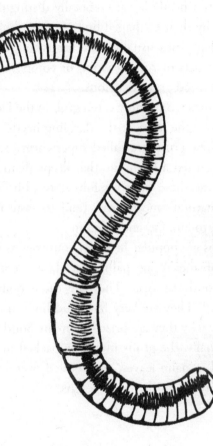

Earthworm

Grub

A grub is a beetle larva. Generally distinguishable from cat-erpillars by their C-shaped bodies, most grubs are edible. I've found that grubs usually taste something like whatever they eat, be it oats or rotting wood or compost. Yet some people still find wood grubs delicious.

The most commonly eaten grub in the United States is the mealworm, the larva of the darkling beetle. Very large varie-ties of these grubs are called superworms, which have some-times been fed a hormone that keeps them larval and grow-ing. I think these latter versions taste a bit fishy, and the very small, "natural" mealworms tend to taste nuttier. Both are high in protein, fat, and calcium.

Grubs are popular in Asian countries as well. Sago grubs, larvae of the Asian palm weevil, are considered delight-ful in Southeast Asia. They are eaten boiled, baked, fried, or roasted. They are very fatty and high in calories, which is probably why they are prized by many Southeast Asian tribes. Traditionally, the grubs might be packed in sago palm flour, wrapped in palm leaves, and roasted over a fire. I think they taste a lot like mushy potato chips.

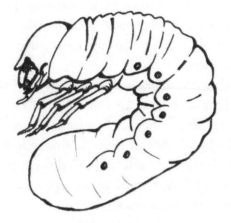

Beetle grub

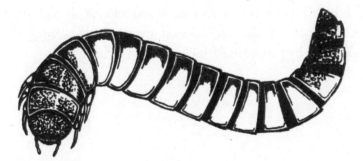

Mealworm

Grasshopper

Grasshoppers—and locusts, their swarming phase—are enjoyed the world over. Popular in Mexico, Asia, Africa, and the Middle East, they are perhaps the most commonly eaten insects on the planet.

Known as *chapulines* in Mexico, they are flavored with *chile* and lime and eaten as a snack or in tacos. In Southeast Asia and China, they are frequently served fried in market stalls. In Japan, they are collected from rice paddies, marinated in soy sauce and sugar, and called *inago*. In Uganda and Kenya, *nsenene*, long-horned grasshoppers (a.k.a. katydids), are a much-valued fried snack.

Grasshoppers come in many different colors. Often, when cooked, they turn red due to the antioxidant pigment astaxanthin in their exoskeleton.

Locusts are actually short-horned grasshoppers. When these grasshoppers sense that their population is high, they transform from shy, antisocial animals into larger, more colorful, highly social organisms that swarm and eat all vegetation in their path. Traditionally, locust swarms have been caught and eaten by people in Africa and the Middle East.

Short-horned grasshopper

Fly

There are dozens of species of edible fly, and they are eaten at all stages of life. The edibility of most flies is determined by their diet. Houseflies themselves are quite edible, though not if they've been feeding on rotting garbage. Housefly pupae taste like blood sausage and are high in iron.

Many species of lake fly are edible, and historically have been collected and relished by native peoples. Certain Northern Paiute Indians of the salty Mono Lake called themselves the Kucadikadi, or "brine fly pupae eaters." Women used woven winnowing baskets to scoop the fly pupae out of the water. The pupae were then mixed with acorns and pine nuts, stirred into soups and stews, or ground with flour to make bread.*

In East Africa, millions of midge flies are caught in nets, ground to paste, pressed into blocks, and then cooked into a nutritious food called Kunga Cake. Aztec caviar, or *ahuauhtli* (pronounced *ah-wa-OOT-lee*), which means "amaranth of the water," consisted of fly eggs[†] harvested from Lake Texcoco. These were said to have a shrimp-like flavor, and were dried and pressed into bricks, or mixed into tortillas or tamales.

Researchers are studying the potential of soldier fly larvae to convert waste like compost into protein for livestock and possibly humans.

---

* Bishop Paiute Tribe newsletter, February 2013.
† And/or water boatman eggs.

Crane fly

Housefly larva

Soldier fly larva

Scorpion

Scorpions look terrifying. But they can be great eating. Just ask the Chinese, who serve them on skewers. Personally, I think they taste like a light, earthy version of crab.

Scorpions, of course, are not insects, but arachnids. Unlike their aquatic, scavenging brethren, they hunt and feed on live insects. Like humans, scorpions give birth to live young.

Unless you are familiar with the nuances of scorpion species, it can be tough to tell the very venomous, dangerous ones from the not-so-dangerous ones. Emperor scorpions, which are the species most commonly kept as pets, have a mild sting, but also a very thick exoskeleton. It's safest to remove the stinger entirely before cooking and eating any scorpion.

Scorpions can be quite long-lived and are important predators in the wild. Take this, and your own safety, into consideration before capturing and eating one. However, better to eat it than squash it, I say.

Scorpion

Tarantula

Tarantulas are beautiful, generally harmless animals, despite being vigorously reviled by much of the population. NASA scientist Mark Rober did an experiment in which he put a rubber turtle, snake, and tarantula on the shoulder of a road to see who would swerve off and hit them. Most drivers ignored them, but the majority of the "cold-blooded rubber animal killers" aimed for the tarantula.

"Tarantulas, I'm going to be honest: You need a new PR firm," he says in the YouTube video documenting his experiment.

Tarantulas tend to taste somewhat like smoky lobster, and are eaten primarily in Cambodia.

Most tarantulas are not poisonous, with bites about as painful as a bee sting. Even a dead tarantula can be harmful, however, as some of them have urticating (think: irritating) hairs on their abdomens, which they kick at those threatening them. When preparing a tarantula, it's safest to either thoroughly burn off these hairs or remove the abdomen entirely, once the animal has been humanely killed. Then be sure to burn the rest of the hairs off the body. After thoroughly cooking the tarantula, carefully remove the fangs from the chelicerae before eating.

Like scorpions, tarantulas are long-lived, important predators.

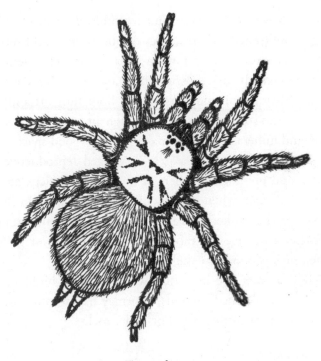

Tarantula

Termite

Although we in the West tend to think of them only once they've infiltrated the structures of our houses, wild termites have been popular as a human food source since before we were human. In places where they are most abundant, like Africa, they remain popular among both humans and apes. Nutty-tasting when toasted, and high in essential fats, protein, and minerals, termites make a mighty good snack.

In many places, the alates, or winged reproductive pre-queen and pre-king members of the termite society, are captured and eaten when they fly off from their nests in droves. However, the worker class are also eaten, fished out from their homes via the age-old moistened stick method, or gathered when their mounds are dug up.

If you don't live in Africa, where termites build impressive, air-conditioned mounds, you may find termite colonies in forests, near rotting wood or under rocks.

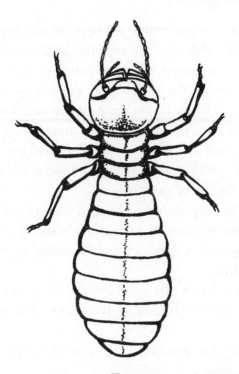

Termite

Wood Louse

Also known as roly-polies, pill bugs, or sow bugs, wood lice are actually neither lice nor any other kind of insect but rather terrestrial crustaceans related to shrimp and crab. A related deep-sea species, the giant isopod, can grow to be more than a foot long. Wood lice in the genus *Armadillidium* can roll into a ball when threatened, like an armadillo, though not all wood lice can do this. They are often confused with the pill millipede, which, unlike the wood louse, tends to have light bands at the tips of its segments.

In *Why Not Eat Insects?* Vincent Holt writes that "wood-louse sauce is equal, if not distinctly superior to, shrimp." There are many recipes for wood lice online, especially on foraging websites.

Folklore has it that wood lice can be eaten to ease stomachaches, perhaps because of the calcium carbonate in their shells.

Due to their crustacean roots, wood lice are often found in moist areas.

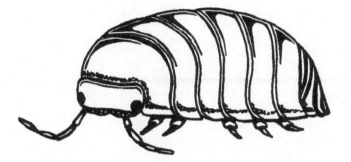

Wood louse

Delectable Edible Insect Recipes

WAX MOTH TACO

SALTY-SWEET WAX WORMS

HAKUNA FRITTATA

CRICKETY KALE SALAD

CICADAS AND ASPARAGUS WITH AIOLI

CIRCLE OF LIFE CANAPÉ

ALMOST AZTEC SHAKE

CRICKET LEATHER

SWEET-N-SPICY SUMMER JUNE BUGS

FLORENCE'S FORTIFIED BROWNIES

A Note on Cooking Insects

WARNING: IF YOU ARE ALLERGIC TO SHELLFISH, BE AWARE
THAT EATING INSECTS COULD TRIGGER AN ALLERGIC RE-
ACTION. INSECTS AND SHELLFISH ARE CLOSELY RELATED
BIOLOGICALLY.

IF YOU ARE ALLERGIC TO BEE STINGS, DON'T EAT BEES.

There are a few basics when it comes to cooking bugs.

Some people like to make sure they "purge" their bugs for a day or so before preparing them in order to make sure their systems are empty. Others, like me, figure that most of what the bugs ate was probably pretty decent vegetable matter, and still others are lazy and impatient (also like me).

Most insects are best frozen before cooking. This is considered a humane way to kill them. Since they are cold-blooded, their nervous systems simply slow down in the freezer, and they go into a deep sleep from which they never awaken. Unlike you or I, warm-blooded mammals who would be very uncomfortable in the cold, animals like insects are designed to go into a form of hibernation. I'm told it's possible for some very hardy species to wake up from an ice nap of several weeks and reanimate, but I've never seen it happen in my own kitchen.

Some cooks like to thoroughly boil their bug bounty before further preparations, though forager Paul Landkamer tells me that purists say rinsing or preboiling removes distinctively flavored pheromones. Personally, I rinse, but I rarely boil insects before preparing them. However, I once watched *Creepy Crawly Cuisine* author Julieta Ramos-Elorduy make a batch of cricket stir-fry, the main ingredient of which she intentionally did not rinse first. I have to say, it was delicious.

To summarize: Freeze first. Preboil or don't. Rinse, probably.

The three most common ways to prepare insects are toasting, sautéing, and frying.

Toasting most closely approximates what our ancestors likely did, via fires, stone ovens, and sun-drying. Toasted insects can then be ground into a nutritious flour.

Sautéing tends to work best with the juvenile, soft-shelled insects such as larvae and young crickets.

Almost every kind of bug, like almost every other food, is good fried.

The safest bet is to order your insects live from a farm. If you collect them from the wild, be aware of the environmental balance. Don't collect too many from one place.

"While gathering ingredients for my dishes, I try to follow what is known as the one-in-twenty rule," says David George Gordon in *The Eat-a-Bug Cookbook*. "I'll take an arthropod only if I am confident there are twenty of the same type nearby."

Do try to make sure that your bugs haven't ingested toxic plants or chemicals.

There is always some risk of toxicity or parasites when eating insects, just as there is with eating any other kind of meat (and even some vegetables—spinach *E. coli,* anyone?). Cook all insects thoroughly before eating. I'll say that again: Cook all insects thoroughly before eating. Forget that *Fear Factor* stuff; eating live insects is just nonsense, not only from a safety standpoint but also from a culinary one. Most bugs taste better cooked. They're kind of like chicken, in that sense at least.

Once bugs are cooked, store them as you would meat.

I've included recipes here not just of my own invention

but also of a few of my friends and colleagues in the entomophagy community who haven't yet published cookbooks
of their own. While the idea of an edible insect recipe may
sound strange, this is just a small sampling of what's available. Edible insect recipes have been around in books since
the 1880s, when Vincent M. Holt published *Why Not Eat Insects?* to help persuade his fellow Victorians to give eating insects a try. Next came *Entertaining with Insects; or, The Original Guide to Insect Cookery* by Ronald L. Taylor and Barbara
J. Carter. The year 1998 saw a boom in the edible bug book
industry, with both *Creepy Crawly Cuisine* by Julieta Ramos-
Elorduy and *The Eat-a-Bug Cookbook* by David George Gordon. In short, I'm rather late to the table, but I've had the
good fortune to benefit from the experience of a lot of great
teachers.

Wax Moth Taco

This is the very first insect dish I ever made, and it remains one of my favorites. During the filming of my first cooking show episode, the producer kept taking laps around the studio, taking a bite of the wax worm filling on every lap until they were gone. When I made them for the documentary "Bug People" by Paul Meyers, the camerawoman, who had never eaten a bug before in her life, said they were "better than chicken." I've had kids fight each other for these. I once brought them to a party where the only person who didn't have seconds was the one who swore he'd never eat a bug—he only had one serving.

Without further ado . . .

> **1 cup wax worms**
> **1 cup chopped onions**
> **2 tbsp olive oil**
> **Pinch of salt**
> **Hot sauce**
> **Tortillas, chopped tomato, chopped cilantro, hot sauce, or whatever else you enjoy with your tacos**

Freeze live wax worms overnight.

Sauté onions in olive oil until golden, then turn heat to medium-high. Add wax worms, stirring quickly to keep them moving, while adding a pinch of salt to taste. Wax worms will start to straighten out as they hit the heat; this means they are partially done and are becoming firm, just like shrimp or fish. When you start to see a little bit of transparency around their edges, they are ready.

Simply use sautéed wax worms as you would any other taco meat, adding whichever complementary ingredients you fancy.

Salty-Sweet Wax Worms

Everyone likes this dish. If I had a very squeamish diner and only one chance to prove how tasty and inoffensive edible insects are, this would be it. It's slightly sweet, slightly salty, crunchy and light as puffed rice, but with a savory nuttiness. It's great as a snack by itself or as a topping drizzled over salad, popcorn, or ice cream. You can also ditch the last step and just eat the crispy caterpillars straight out of the oven (once they've cooled off, of course).

> **Wax worms**
> **Sugar**
> **Salt**

Spread thawed wax worms on a baking pan. They have enough fat in them that they don't usually need any kind of oil, but you can add a light greasing to the pan first if you wish.

Roast wax worms at 350°F until crispy and golden, about 5 minutes. Shake pan occasionally to rotate wax worms. If you hear them pop, that's okay—it's just the sound of them getting crispy. Keep a close eye on them. They are small, and can go from being done to being burned very quickly.

Toss crisped wax worms in a hot pan with a dash each of sugar and salt. Keep them moving. Sugar should melt and stick to wax worms. Remove and place in a bowl.

That's it! I like to get creative and experiment with different flavors and spices, such as wasabi powder, ginger powder, or chipotle powder. Just toss the candied wax worms in a bowl with a dash of the spice of your choosing. If you find a really good combo, let me know!

Hakuna Frittata

The phrase *hakuna matata* is Swahili for "no worries." It was popularized by Disney's *The Lion King* in a song sung by the now famously insectivorous duo Timon and Pumbaa—a meerkat and a warthog, respectively. During the song, they try to teach Simba, a lion cub, the wisdom of their carefree life of bug eating. No more running down big game. Just knock on a log to find some grub.

Simba's reaction to slurping his first larva is "slimy yet satisfying." I'm confident your reviews for the following dish will be considerably more positive. The nutty mushroom flavor of the wax worms blends perfectly with the actual mushrooms, and the insects would add protein and essential fatty acids. Timon and Pumbaa would be drooling with envy.

4 eggs
½ cup milk
1 tbsp butter
½ chopped onion
1 cup chopped oyster mushrooms (I prefer king oyster
mushrooms, often found at Asian markets)
Salt
Splash of white wine
½ cup wax worms
Pepper
½ cup grated Gruyère cheese
Fresh thyme (optional)

Beat eggs and milk together in a bowl.

Melt butter in frying pan. Sauté onions until they begin to soften, then add mushrooms. Salt lightly to help draw out liquid. When mushrooms soften, add splash of cooking wine. Toss ingredients quickly until wine has evaporated. When mushrooms begin to brown, add the wax worms. Continue sautéing, flipping occasionally (if you can) until wax worms become firm and slightly golden at edges.

Pour eggs and milk into frying pan. Add a dash of salt and pepper. Cook until nearly firm, then remove from stovetop and sprinkle with grated Gruyère. Place under broiler for 2 to 4 minutes until cheese is golden. Slice into triangles. Serve with sprig of fresh thyme.

Crickety Kale Salad

You say you don't like kale? I'll make you eat your words. This is my go-to potluck dish (admittedly, sans crickets in mixed company—I don't force my ento-enthusiasm on everyone), and I never come home with leftovers or without being asked for the recipe. For the more open-minded eater, the crickets add a nutty crunch, a garlicky zing, and a healthy dose of protein, iron, and calcium.

CRICKET TOPPING

> 1 tsp olive oil
> ¾ cup crickets
> 1 clove garlic, crushed; OR garlic salt
> Salt

SALAD

> 1 bunch kale
> ¼ cup olive oil
> Juice of ½ lemon
> Salt, garlic salt, and chipotle powder
> ½ avocado
> ½ cup cranberries
> Pine nuts (optional)

Heat oven to 350°F. Use 1 tsp olive oil to grease a baking pan. Toss rinsed, thawed crickets in a bowl with crushed garlic and dash of salt (or just garlic salt). Spread crickets evenly out on baking sheet. Bake for 5 to 10 minutes or until crispy and golden, turning occasionally with a spatula.

Chop rinsed, dried kale into bite-sized pieces, and place in large salad bowl. Pour 1/4 cup olive oil over leaves, then gently work hands through leaves, "massaging" the oil into the surfaces of the leaves. This needn't take long—it's mainly to make sure the oil is evenly distributed throughout the kale.

Add the lemon juice, and sprinkle on a dash of salt, garlic salt, and chipotle powder. Toss thoroughly, or work through with hands.

Top with chopped avocado, cranberries, garlicky crickets, and optional pine nuts.

Cicadas and Asparagus with Aioli

This was a crowd pleaser at a recent event at the Dutch embassy in Washington, DC, at the tail end of the seventeen-year cicada emergence of 2013. University of Maryland entomology professor and BugOfTheWeek.com author Mike Raupp brought in foraged cicadas, just as he had a few weeks prior for his segment on *The Tonight Show with Jay Leno.* Raupp offered Leno a dollar if he ate one, and the host promptly popped one in his mouth.

"Delicious!" he declared, and I think you'll agree.

If you can't get hold of cicadas, any other large insect would do: Grasshoppers, big mealworms (a.k.a. superworms), or dragonflies come to mind.

> 1 bunch asparagus, trimmed
> Olive oil
> 1 cup cicadas
> 1–2 cloves garlic
> Salt
> Toothpicks
> Parsley for garnish

AIOLI

> ¾ cup mayonnaise
> 3 tbsp lemon juice
> 3 cloves garlic
> ½ tsp salt
> ½ tsp fresh-ground pepper
> Dash of paprika

Blanch asparagus briefly in boiling water until bright green (I like to leave mine crispy). Set aside in a bowl of cold water.

Heat olive oil in a pan. Add in cicadas and 1 to 2 cloves crushed garlic. Sauté with a dash of salt until crispy.

As cicadas cool, cut asparagus spears into inch-and-a-half-long pieces. Skewer one sautéed cicada with one piece of asparagus on each toothpick.

For the aioli, mix the mayonnaise, lemon juice, remaining crushed garlic, salt, and pepper in a small dipping bowl. Sprinkle on a dash of paprika for color.

Arrange canapés on a plate with dipping sauce in the center. Alternatively, add a small dollop of aioli to each cicada. Garnish with parsley.

Circle of Life Canapé

I served this hors d'oeuvre at a banquet for the winners of the United Nations International Year of Forests awards, given by the World Future Council at New York City's Central Park Zoo. With the sounds of seals barking and monkeys hooting in the background, dignitaries from around the world dined on my bug amuse-bouches until they were gone. Longtime vegan, ten-time Olympic medalist, and United Nations Food and Agriculture Organization Goodwill Ambassador Carl Lewis was particularly enthusiastic about them, dragging other people over to make sure they had a taste.

That this recipe includes figs is no accident. Figs and bugs—wasps, specifically—have an intimate, long-standing symbiotic relationship. These two species grew up together, have co-evolved in an intricate dance of interdependency for more than seventy million years. Each sweet fruit represents a labor of love and the ultimate sacrifice for one of the dancers.

In order to get pollinated, fig trees have developed an inverted flower—i.e., the fig—into which a female wasp must crawl in order to lay her eggs, pollinating the flower in the process.* Unfortunately for the wasp, her wings get ripped off in the narrow entry passage, and she is digested by the fig's enzymes, her nutrients absorbed into the fruit. She not only pollinates the flower; she also becomes part of the fig itself. In this sense, all figs have a wasp within them.

If she has managed to lay her eggs in the correct spot, the fig protects her young until they mature enough to leave of their own volition. Once emerged, the wasps mate (so that act is in your fig as well). After mating, the male wasps, wingless but with sharp teeth, chew their way out of the fig, then die. Their deaths are not in vain, for they've made way for the winged females, who fly off to begin the cycle again.

---

* Remember, pollen is essentially plant sperm. The wasp is inseminating the fig flower as she is laying her own eggs.

Each fig canapé represents this cycle, with an insect at the heart of the fig and the cheese, a symbol of the mother wasp's sacrifice, centered in the protective womb of the fig.

If you could get hold of wasp larvae, they would be a great topping for this dish, but as they can be hard to come by, I've substituted grasshoppers instead.

> 6 fresh figs
> Butter
> ¼ tsp ground sage
> ¼ tsp ground thyme
> ¼ tsp ground marjoram
> ¼ tsp ground oregano (if you don't have all of these, a mix of other herbs will suffice)
> Salt, to taste
> Pepper, to taste
> Chèvre
> 1 dozen grasshoppers (large crickets will work fine)

Slice figs lengthwise, preserving the stems. Gently squeeze figs vertically between thumb and forefingers so that the center of the fig opens up. Set aside.

Heat a thin layer of butter in a frying pan. Mix the ground herbs, and sprinkle in 1/2 tsp of the mixture and a dash of salt and pepper. When butter is sizzling, place figs face down in the butter for a minute or so. Remove and set aside, face up. Spoon a small dollop of the chèvre into the hole in the center.

Heat more butter in same frying pan, and sauté grasshoppers with a dash of the herb mixture for about three minutes. Remove.

Place one grasshopper atop each fig-chèvre mound. Enjoy!

Almost Aztec Shake

A collaboration between Dianne Guilfoyle of BugMuscle and myself, this recipe includes a powerful punch of protein, essential fatty acids, iron, and calcium.

Most of the ingredients are Aztec in origin: Peanuts, vanilla, cocoa, and insects were all part of the Aztec diet. Of course, the dairy products are an exception.

½ cup roasted or dried mealworms and crickets
½ cup peanut butter
1 scoop low-fat vanilla ice cream
2 cups low-fat milk
1 banana
1 tbsp cocoa powder

Blend or grind the toasted bugs until they are as fine a powder as possible. Set the protein powder aside.

Mix together all ingredients, adding protein powder in last.

Cricket Leather

The first time I tasted John Heylin's Cricket Leather was at a "Nerd Nite" event in a nightclub in San Francisco. I wasn't the only patron vying for seconds of this nutty-sweet, protein-packed treat, and they were all gone in a flash.

The Cricket Leather was an example of a product that could be made with the organic, dried cricket flour John plans to produce through his company, Chirp Inc. Chirp's vision is to create solar-powered "cricket apartments" in shipping containers in Oakland, California, and then to process the flour on-site. They shelled out for a special milling machine, which produces an ultrafine flour, but you can approximate this at home with a blender. Your cricket flour may not be as smooth as a professionally milled one, but it will still be very tasty.

1 cup chopped apples
½ cup cranberries
¼ cup cricket flour
Honey, to taste

EQUIPMENT

Baking sheet
Oven/dehydrator
Blender/coffee grinder
Sifter
Parchment paper

Cricket Flour

Heat oven to 350°F. Spread frozen crickets evenly across a lightly oiled baking sheet. Bake for 5 to 10 minutes until very crispy, rotating crickets with a spatula every few minutes. When they are ready, you should be able to crush one easily between your fingers like a Rice Krispy.

Place toasted crickets into a blender or coffee grinder, and grind until powdered. Sift out the bigger bits for a smoother result, or keep them in for crunch.

Leather

Put apples, cranberries, cricket flour, and a little water in a blender and then puree. Add honey until it reaches the level of sweetness you desire. Put parchment paper on a baking sheet and then spread the puree out evenly on the paper. Heat oven to 140°F and put in baking sheet. Cook for roughly 8 hours, or until it is no longer sticky to the touch. Remove and enjoy!

Sweet-n-Spicy Summer June Bugs

Paul Landkamer, avid entomophagy teacher and intrepid taster of wild edibles, recently sent me a box of his latest six-legged culinary creations. There were raspberry-glazed cicadas, sweet pickled grasshoppers, seasoned stinkbugs, and a few other goodies, but my favorites were his spicy-sweet june bugs.

If you've ever seen june bugs gathering in the summertime, with their brown shells and buzzing wings, you might not think they look very appetizing. But research chemist/foraging instructor Mark "Merriwether" Vorderbruggen notes that they have been appreciated as the tasty morsels they are for hundreds of years.

"Native Americans simply tossed them onto hot coals and when they 'popped' they were done," he says. "Pulling off the wings and legs leaves you with a walnutty-sweet golden lump of protein and fat."

Catching them is easy. Since they are nocturnal and highly attracted to light, Vorderbruggen recommends hanging up a white sheet and shining a flashlight at it. When the bugs come to the spotlight, you grab them, or brush them off into a container.

"They are easily recognized, don't bite or sting, and have no similar-looking poisonous mimics," he says.

However, it is important to remember that they are wild, and it's not always possible to tell what they have been munching on. If the leaves they've been eating were sprayed with pesticides, you may be ingesting those, too. Thus, it's best to collect them in a rural area.

After collecting and freezing the bugs overnight, Landkamer boils them for 10 to 15 minutes before further preparing them. Alternatively, he says, "if you're going to cook them immediately, substitute boiling for a quick rinse to get dirt and plant matter washed off."

1 can (14 oz) jellied cranberry sauce
2 tbsp brown sugar

4 tsp garlic powder
1 tsp ground red pepper
1 tsp ground ginger
1 tbsp cumin
Preboiled june bugs
Sweet-n-Spicy Sauce

Stir or blend cranberry sauce, brown sugar, garlic powder, red pepper, ginger, and cumin till well mixed, thinning with water as necessary.

Marinate a bunch of june bugs in the Sweet-n-Spicy Sauce overnight. Spread them out in a single layer on dehydrator pans and dehydrate overnight, or 24 hours, till they have hardened substantially. They'll never be perfectly crispy due to the sugar, but they will come a long way. They peel most easily from the pan if you chill the pan first.

Florence's Fortified Brownies

Dr. Florence Dunkel is, in many ways, the mother of the modern entomophagy movement in America. In 1995 she took over running the *Food Insects Newsletter,* an online source for entomophagy information.

An entomology professor at Montana State University, Florence has been serving insects to her students and the public for more than a decade. *Fear Factor* solicited, then largely ignored, her advice on how to serve insects, thus the grimaces on the faces of the contestants.

Florence travels frequently to Africa, where she has observed insect eating in its traditional setting. One of the most moving moments for her was a night in Mali when she observed little children running through the street, catching grasshoppers.

That the children catch and eat insects there is an important microcosm of their culture. The kids get together to make bug-catching bags, then hone their hunting skills filling them up. Next, they borrow stoves from their parents to cook their bounty, which they then share with other children. The whole cycle is part of their journey into adulthood.

These brownies might be an easy way to sneak some extra protein, calcium, and iron into your kids' dessert, tying them to this ancient way of life and learning about food. Make enough to share!

This brownie recipe was adapted from *Betty Crocker's New Picture Cook Book,* 1961, first edition. All the adaptations are Florence's, tested by about a thousand students and guests over the past fifteen years.

Prepare the fortification.
You can use roasted crickets, but the fortification Florence prefers is with toasted or butter-sautéed Tenebrio (mealworms). This is substituted for nuts in the following recipe. After the Tenebrio are sautéed or toasted, finely chop or

chop in a blender (toasted Tenebrio work best with the latter method). Set aside and prepare the rest of the brownies.

Assemble ingredients for the brownies.

2 squares unsweetened chocolate (2 oz); or substitute
3 tbsp cocoa + 1 tbsp butter for 1 square unsweetened
chocolate
⅓ cup shortening or butter
1 cup sugar
2 eggs
¾ cup flour
½ tsp baking powder
½ tsp salt
½ cup roasted insects

Prepare the brownies.

Heat oven to 350°F. Grease a square pan, 8 × 8 × 2 inches. Melt chocolate and shortening over hot water (double boiler works best). Beat in sugar and eggs. Blend flour, baking powder, and salt; stir in. Mix in roasted insects. Spread in pan.

Bake 30 to 35 minutes or until slight imprint remains when touched lightly with finger. Cool slightly and cut into squares. If desired, spread with Florence's Chocolate Frosting (below) before cutting. Makes 16 two-inch squares.

Frost with Florence's Chocolate Frosting.

Whip 1/2 cup room-temperature butter with 1 to 2 cups confectioner's sugar and 1/2 cup cocoa; add 1 tbsp cream if needed, plus 1 tsp of flavoring such as vanilla or mint extract. Whip until smooth. Spread over cooled brownies.

As Florence says, "Bug appétit!"

Bibliography

Bodenheimer, F. S. *Insects as Human Food.* The Hague: Dr. W. Junk Publishers, 1951.

Bryant, Edwin. *What I Saw in California.* New York: D. Appleton & Company, 1848.

Cordain, Loren. *The Paleo Diet: Lose Weight and Get Healthy by Eating the Foods You Were Designed to Eat.* Revised edition. Hoboken, N.J.: John Wiley & Sons, 2011.

Corson, Trevor. *The Story of Sushi: An Unlikely Saga of Raw Fish and Rice.* New York: Harper Perennial, 2008.

Dahlberg, Frances, ed. *Woman the Gatherer.* New Haven and London: Yale University Press, 1981.

Daniel, Kaayla T. *The Whole Soy Story: The Dark Side of America's Favorite Health Food.* Washington, DC: New Trends Publishing Inc., 2005.

DeFoliart, Gene, Florence Vaccarello Dunkel, and David Gracer, eds. *The Food Insects Newsletter: Chronicle of a Changing Culture.* Salt Lake City: Aardvark Global Publishing Company, 2009.

Durst, Patrick B., Dennis V. Johnson, Robin N. Leslie, and Kenichi Shono, eds. *Forest Insects: Humans Bite Back.* Bangkok: Food and Agriculture Organization of the United Nations, Regional Office for Asia and the Pacific, 2010.

George, Kathryn Paxton. *Animal, Vegetable, or Woman?: A Feminist Critique of Ethical Vegetarianism.* Albany: State University of New York Press, 2000.

Gordon, David George. *The Eat-a-Bug Cookbook: 40 Ways to Cook Crick-*

ets, Grasshoppers, Ants, Waterbugs, Spiders, Centipedes, and Their Kin. New York: Ten Speed Press, 2013.

Harris, Marvin. *Food and Evolution: Toward a Theory of Human Food Habits.* Philadelphia: Temple University Press, 1989.

Holt, Vincent M. *Why Not Eat Insects?* London: Field & Tuer, the Leadenhall Press, E.C., 1885.

Keith, Lierre. *The Vegetarian Myth: Food, Justice, and Sustainability.* Crescent City, CA: Flashpoint Press, 2009.

Kingsolver, Barbara. *Animal, Vegetable, Miracle: A Year of Food Life.* New York: HarperCollins Publishers, 2007.

Lauck, Joanne Elizabeth. *The Voice of the Infinite in the Small: Re-Visioning the Insect-Human Connection.* Mill Spring, NC: Swan-Raven & Co, 1998.

Menzel, Peter, and Faith D'Aluisio. *Man Eating Bugs: The Art and Science of Eating Insects.* Berkeley, CA: Ten Speed Press, 1998.

Paoletti, Maurizio G., ed. *Ecological Implications of Minilivestock: Potential of Insects, Rodents, Frogs and Snails.* Enfield, NH: Science Publishers Inc., 2005.

Pollan, Michael. *The Omnivore's Dilemma: A Natural History of Four Meals.* New York: The Penguin Group, 2006.

Pritzker, Barry M. *A Native American Encyclopedia: History, Culture, and People.* New York: Oxford University Press, 2000.

Ramos-Elorduy, Julieta. *Creepy Crawly Cuisine: The Gourmet Guide to Edible Insects.* South Paris, ME: Park Street Press, 1998.

Taylor, Ronald L. *Butterflies in My Stomach: Or, Insects in Human Nutrition.* Santa Barbara, CA: Woodbridge Press, 1975.

Taylor, Ronald L., and Barbara J. Carter. *Entertaining with Insects.* Santa Barbara, CA: Woodbridge Press, 1976.

U.S. Food and Drug Administration. *Defect Levels Handbook: Levels of Natural or Unavoidable Defects in Foods That Present No Health Hazards for Humans.* Updated June 17, 2013. http://www.fda.gov/Food/Guidance Regulation/GuidanceDocumentsRegulatoryInformation/Sanitation Transportation/ucm056174.htm.

Van Huis, Arnold, Joost Van Itterbeeck, Harmke Klunder, Esther Mertens, Afton Halloran, Giulia Muir, and Paul Vantomme. "Edible Insects: Future Prospects for Food and Feed Security." Food and Agriculture Organization of the United Nations. http://www.fao.org/docrep/018/i3253e/i3253e.pdf.

About the Author

© James Rollyson

Daniella Martin first became fascinated with insect cuisine while conducting anthropological fieldwork in the Yucatán, Mexico. Since then she has become a verified entomophagist, or bug-eating expert, and speaks frequently at places such as the Natural History Museum of Los Angeles, NASA, New York's Central Park Zoo, and the California Academy of Sciences, among others. Daniella blogs for the *Huffington Post* and has been featured in many publications, including the 2011 *New Yorker* article "Grub: Eating Bugs to Save the Planet," the *Wall Street Journal*, *SF Weekly*, *Women's Health*, AOL News, and TreeHugger.com. Her favorite insects to eat are wax worms, bees, wasps, and fried bamboo worms.

www.girlmeetsbug.com